I dedicate this book to

AZIM PREMJI

an amazing, self-effacing, generous, altruistic person with an impressive demeanour and nobility of character. His magnanimous donation of USD 21 billion towards education makes him the third-largest donor in the world and the largest donor in India. A patriotic Indian-Muslim, he has made his community and India proud.

'I strongly believe that those of us, who are privileged to have wealth, should contribute significantly to try and create a better world for the millions who are far less privileged.'
— Azim Premji

ASSALAMUALAIKUM WATAN

Sanjay Khan

FiNGERPRINT!

Published by
FiNGERPRINT!
An imprint of Prakash Books India Pvt. Ltd.

113/A, Darya Ganj, New Delhi-110 002,
Tel: (011) 2324 7062 – 65, Fax: (011) 2324 6975
Email: info@prakashbooks.com/sales@prakashbooks.com

www.facebook.com/fingerprintpublishing
www.twitter.com/FingerprintP
www.fingerprintpublishing.com

Copyright © 2020 Prakash Books India Pvt. Ltd.
Copyright Text © Sanjay Khan

All rights reserved. No part of this publication may be reproduced, stored in a retrieval system or transmitted in any form or by any means, electronic, mechanical, photocopying, recording or otherwise (except for mentions in reviews or edited excerpts in the media) without the written permission of the publisher.

ISBN: 978 93 8971 733 4

Processed & printed in India

Long time ago I asked my good friend the late Atal Bihari Vajpayee ji, former prime minister of India, "What is the best way forward for India?" He, quickly and in no uncertain terms, replied, "The only way forward for India is secularism; there is no other way."

Atal Bihari Vajpayee to Sanjay Khan
on the sets of *The Great Maratha* in 1995

NOTE OF THANKS

Firstly, I would like to express my deep gratitude to the People of India who have always been an inspiration of my life's journey; all throughout I was blessed with their love, affection, and concern. *Assalamualaikum Watan* is a book I dedicate to my country and my parents whose values I cherish till date. The spirit of secularism and unity has inspired my passion to bring this book out at a time I feel is appropriate. Today, I see our nation on the verge of becoming a superpower, however, it's my personal view that our great country is a major factor in the growth of the world economy. My life has been a giant explosion of creative aspirations and achievements; the culture and history of our great nation has been a driving force in my life; over the years I have always tried to inspire the youth about its importance and place in our lives and will continue to do so till the last breath of my life.

My tryst with history is one of the strong pillars of my personality; I have always been a flag-bearer of peace and harmony. I've delved deep in the research for this book to bring few important aspects which have been swept under the carpet from public view and I strongly feel it is a threat to our nation's fabric to do so, as many historians would like to agree with me that 'bad history' affects our youth and development. As an Indian I felt it was my duty to place these facts of history for the greater understanding of our people, as this would cure the minds of faulty judgements.

Assalamualaikum Watan is a call to my Muslim brothers and sisters to come and contribute to the building of this nation and join the mainstream to consider themselves as one amongst the equals and definitely not an outsider. It does not preach an ideology but reminds one of those great Muslim achievers whose contributions have made India a citadel of peace, harmony, and secularism in spite of its vast diversity. The strength of Islam in India can only add to its progress and development. The Quran provides implicitly that the loyalty of the citizen is dedicated to the land they eat the salt from.

I genuinely thank my readers who made my previous book, *The Best Mistakes of My Life,* a best-seller, which inspired me to write this book. My wife Zarine has been a driving force who stood with me through the storms of life. I am proud of my children Farah, Simone, Sussanne, Zayed, and Mallika, who accept all my values and practice them to the best of their abilities and become the achievers they are. My deep affection to Aqeel Ali, Ajay Arora, my sons-in-law, and Hrithik Roshan, the father of my grandchildren.

I express my love to all my grandchildren Azaan Ali, Fizaa Ali, Armaan Arora, Yuraaz Arora, Adah Arora, Hrehaan Roshan, Hridaan Roshan, Zidaan Khan, and Aariz Khan. I remember my late brother Feroz Khan with deep affection, and my late sister Khurshid, may peace be upon them, as well as my brothers Sameer, Shahrukh, Akbar, and my loving sister Dilshad.

I am most grateful to the friends who came forward in helping me complete my work on *Assalamualaikum Watan*.

My grateful thanks to Late Dr M Rehman (IAS, Former Secretary, Government of India), Dr Asad M Madni (Distinguished Professor, University of California, Los Angeles and Fellow, US National Academy of Engineering), Vikram Mehta (Chief Executive Officer, Shell India), Jamal A Madni (Managing Director, Enterprise Technology Strategy, The Boeing Company), Syed Shahid Mehdi (Retired IAS, Former Vice-Chancellor, Jamia Millia Islamia University), Maqbool Nikat Mehdi (MA, Urdu literature), Vijay Karan (Former Director, CBI), Mohammed Khan, (Chairman, Enterprise Nexus Communications), Malvika Sanghvi (eminent journalist), Professor Azizuddin Husain (History department, Jamia Millia Islamia University). Then there is Margaret Peacock for her valuable comments, Anirban Dutta Gupta for his extended co-operation, Suhail Mathur of The Book Bakers for publishing advice as the litery agent, Imran ibn

Abdulla, Athar ibn Abdulla (Inhead) for the cover page artwork, Daboo Ratnani for the front-page picture of myself, Rajesh Rajput for the research material, the trailer and his whole-hearted efforts in compiling the book.

And lastly Shikha Sabharwal (Publishing Director) and Pooja Dadwal (Managing Editor) of Fingerprint! Publishing for their trust on my creative instinct and publishing *Assalamualaikum Watan*.

FOREWORD

Rarely, if ever, does the life of an actor, director, or a movie producer parallel the legendary roles that he or she portrays on the big screen. Sanjay Khan, a veteran actor, movie-maker, television producer, author, and entrepreneur is just such a person.

From the days of his young adulthood, he was determined to find a medium of self-expression that also contributed to the awareness of society. It did not take him long to realize that the natural convergence of his two desires was films. This calling resulted in an extraordinary career that spanned across forty-seven films as a leading actor. During the course of his personal and professional evolution, he realized that he wanted to contribute to more than just entertainment; he wanted to be a messenger of social, moral, and ethical ideals.

He must have found a strong resonance in movies such as *Chandi Sona*, which had an all-encompassing theme of compassion to those physically challenged and in need of protection, empathy, and respect; in *Abdullah*, which was centred on the values of communal harmony intertwined with national integration; and in the beautifully crafted *Kala Dhanda Gore Log*, which dealt with the subject of drug trafficking and its effects on the youth of India.

One of Sanjay's greatest concerns, however, has always been the plight of his Muslim brothers and sisters in India. This resulted in his epic TV serial, *The Sword of Tipu Sultan*, through which he wished to convey a message to the Muslim community to ignite in their hearts the zeal, passion, and urgency to reclaim their rightful place in India. *Tipu Sultan* was one of the biggest successes of its time and was highly appreciated and acclaimed by both Muslims and Hindus alike.

As Sanjay so eloquently stated himself, "As an artist, to remain outside the abstract world of meticulous creation and be ensconced in the spirit from the lives touched by my art was one of the greatest satisfactions and humbling moments of my life."

During his legendary career, he accomplished what most people can only dream of. A successful movie mogul, entrepreneur, and family man, Sanjay has earned the respect and admiration of world leaders, including prime ministers, kings, maharajas, scientists, and other leading personalities who have befriended him for life. The question now arises, "What does he have left to prove?" To answer this, it is important to recognize that the plight of his Muslim brothers and sisters in India still continues to disturb him and it is this element that has inspired him to conduct an intensive research for his book *Assalamualaikum Watan*.

The book is organized into well-focused sections and chapters, including a brief history of India, highlighting some major contributions of the Indian civilization. It stresses, in particular, on the status of Muslims, being defined as a minority community according to the Constitution of India. Sanjay shares his reservation about this definition since he considers himself an Indian first and then a person of his faith. He does not see himself and his interaction with the rest of society through the narrow prism of religion. It is his view that the terminology 'minority' be dispensed with altogether as it creates the perception of a community that is 'inferior' and is in dire need of 'help' in order to establish itself equal to the 'majority'. He recommends that the Government of India embark on an initiative to address all its citizens as Indians, and in special circumstances, if need be, as Indian-Hindus, Indian-Muslims, Indian-Christians, and so forth.

In summary, Sanjay has produced a book that is most timely, enlightening, and frank. It is well researched and he demonstrates the power of his convictions with his no-holds-barred approach. I believe that every Indian (especially Muslims) should read this work as it will provide a unique perspective of the role the Muslim community has played in the nation-building of India and the potential it has in moulding India's future.

As interesting and valuable as the book is, it is

equally interesting to speculate on the burning desire that drove Sanjay to devote such a major portion of his life in communicating the plight of his Muslim brothers and sisters in India, and in providing a prescription for gradually alleviating this situation. For my part, I believe that after playing larger than life roles on the big screen and with his spiritual awakening in the aftermath of the fire tragedy on the sets of *The Sword of Tipu Sultan*, Sanjay was ready to play the largest role of his life: Sanjay Khan. It seems that Allah, the merciful, the compassionate, has touched his spirit in a special and unique way.

Dr Asad M Madni
Los Angeles, California
2019

PREFACE

It was a hot, dusty summer day at Deoband, Uttar Pradesh, in the year 1990. I slowly walked over to the microphone placed at the far end of the podium, mentally preparing myself to address the huge congregation at the Darul Uloom Deoband. In front of me, looking back expectantly, was a sea of faces, majority of them Indian-Muslims. As I looked at them I was overwhelmed by the knowledge that most of them were disenchanted by the promises of the politicians and other social and religious leaders.

Ever since my teenage years, I have watched the continuous and gradual decline of the Muslim status in India; how blithely promises have been made and how equally easily these have been broken. I have been confounded by the lack of visible leadership, with the exception of a few quasi religio-social and religious organizations who to the best of their abilities have worked and are working towards the upliftment of the

Muslims in India. However, there has been a serious lack of concerted effort to empower this community with the education of technology, commerce, science, and arts, so that they can leverage the power of knowledge and hoist themselves to the heights of success and fulfilment from the dust bowls of society where they have been relegated. They must make this effort, if not for themselves, but for their children and grandchildren and the generations to come.

Through my journeys across the length and breadth of India, I have passed through and paused at numerous Muslim mohallas, and it is with deep anguish and sorrow that I have witnessed the abject poverty and helplessness of the Muslim population, living in squalor and grime. At times I have been ashamed and deeply embarrassed as to how God could give me so much and so little to others . . .

To this date, I remember the vivid scenes from a hovel in one of the mohallas I had stopped at. In the coolness of the night, I heard a father intone in a voice devoid of hope, *"Hamare ghar mein teen din se chula nahin jalaa. Bachhon ko paani pila ke sula dete hum"* (I have not cooked for three days now. I put my children to sleep after giving them some water). The whimper from a hungry child, trying desperately to forget the gnawing in his stomach, tore at my heart. I asked him what his feelings were. "In this state of frustration my mind stops thinking, and I cannot think anymore!" he replied. I asked him his age. 'Forty-five," he said. His gaunt and vacant face looked more like sixty-five.

Outside, on the garbage-filled lanes, I found the

mohalla boys busy playing cricket or gulli-danda. When I posed them a few questions, they responded, maybe not coherently but with immense spirit and optimism. They did try to hide their poverty, but they couldn't hide the attitude and bravado they possessed in abundance. It shone through. One kid said, "*Allah bade hain, sab thik ho jayega*" (Allah is great, everything will be fine).

What is their future, where will they go—the poor, the uneducated, the unemployed—whether Muslim or Hindu? What kind of child will a poor, hungry, uneducated woman bear? What kind of education will she provide the child? What kind of citizens will they become? As Napoleon said: 'Give me an educated mother, I shall promise you the birth of a civilised, educated nation.'

By 2060, Pew Research Centre estimates that there will be more Muslims in India than anywhere else in the world (Indonesia has the most today), and that they will constitute 19% of Indians.[1]

All surveys, including one by World Atlas, indicates that all demography between Hindus and Muslims will grow proportionately, hence the percentage of Hindus will be large and formidable.[2] If we look at this pragmatically, with a good sense of the history of the land, there is no cause for alarm or panic whatsoever.

At the same time, it is my concern that the share of Muslims in the Lok Sabha, India's 545-seat lower house of the Parliament, is in decline. Muslims have always been underrepresented here, but they are currently at a 50-year low. In the 1980 election, almost 10% of those elected were Muslim. In 2014, it was less than 4%, and in 2019 it has marginally increased to 4.95%.

The lack of Muslims in the Lok Sabha will have serious policy consequences. A set of 276,000 questions asked in the Parliament from 1999 to 2017 found that Muslim representatives were far more likely to ask questions about issues that particularly concerned the community, including on violence against Muslims and treatment of Muslim prisoners. The low number of Muslim women—less than 1%—in Lok Sabha means the issues concerning this segment is particularly unlikely to be heard.[3]

Over the decades I have expressed my anguish to many political leaders, both Hindus and Muslims, and each one has assured me that plans have been made, employment created, opportunities generated, so on and so forth. But I have become deaf to this jingoistic jabber by now as I realize that they were mostly paying lip service and it was mostly rhetoric. To me this is worse than genocide. We are letting a community slowly and deliberately die by taking away their pride and self-respect, their opportunity for better livelihood, while waving the flag of false promises.

As I stood in Deoband that day, waiting patiently in front of the mike to let the clamour die down, I said, "Friends, brother, and countrymen! I am not here to give a speech but to talk to you. About you, me, and us. India is a great nation and when you look at the flag, the Indian Tiranga, and see the green in it, remember it represents the Indian-Muslims. So, you all have an equal stake in this country's future! Democracy is not the rule of majority, it is how secure the minority feels. Rise up and be proud citizens of India."

At the end of the address, I was carried on the shoulders of the tumultuous crowd as they ecstatically thundered my name. It was then that I realized the reason behind their rapturous acclaim—I had given them an identity and a pride in who they were and a motivation to achieve and improve themselves.

I had my answer and the path was clear.

SECTION I

ASSALAMUALAIKUM WATAN
'MAY PEACE BE UPON YOU'

The plane was minutes from taking off to Goa from Mumbai, and as I entered and took my seat, my mind was already on my packed itinerary, specially the first meeting of the day. With my face buried in my phone and just a few steps away from being able to rest my legs and recline into my seat, I almost missed seeing a familiar face, that of the industrious and enterprising Nisa Godrej, daughter of my dear friend Adi. As we began exchanging pleasantries and catching up on each other's activities she explained that she was headed to Goa with a group of YPOs, who happened to be sitting just a few feet away. She asked if I would meet them.

As I went around shaking hands and seeing the youthful exuberance, unadulterated idealism, and ambitious restlessness sculpted on all their faces, I couldn't help but realize there was a glaring omission. Of all the youth I met, I noticed there was not a single

Muslim. As the group and I gracefully parted ways, I went back to my seat, reflectively glancing through the window, wondering whether this group was simply an anachronism or a standard representative sample of a deep-seated problem—the absence of Indian-Muslims in mainstream India, in private, social, and governmental functions. By the time the plane touched Goa, I had formulated the intriguing question: Are we Muslims being ignored or are we not equipped to join the mainstream?

It's a simple question and probably one that inflames the incendiary political-religious climate further. But it needs to be looked into. This isn't the first incident I have seen which makes me wonder about this lack of Indian-Muslims in the mainstream of Indian life. It's the nth one that finally makes me say this out loud.

I want to inspire, motivate, and revive our Indian-Muslim society to successfully seek their rightful place in mainstream India. At one point in our illustrious history, Muslims were the first catalysts in creating a united Hindustan, as India was known then, through their genius of discoveries in art and science and investment in a modern economy; they made the entire world envious of India's wealth. That era gave way to a bottomless abyss of mediocrity and apathy, one without any relevant leadership. Till yesterday, our nation's leaders were aimlessly swimming in a pond of bureaucracy instead of crossing the oceans of progress and meeting challenges. I'm saddened that the Indian leadership was parochial and short-sighted in the past decades.

However, the night is dark just before the dawn and the glimmering light of belief for our Indian-Muslims to reclaim the spirit of the soil is now upon us. This book is a message about reclaiming our chutzpa by reviving a mentality through revisiting history, and I can think of no more compelling tale to initially revisit than the on-going story of my life's own transcendent attachments to my nation.

I was at the tender age of seven when the Partition took place, indulging in a youthful admiration for Mahatma Gandhi. I was very fortunate and proud to grow up in a very secular family atmosphere, never once hearing a communal or caste derision at the dinner table. However, religion was a very vital component of our lifestyle; my father was a very religious man and we learned to say our prayers daily. Yet despite being religious in nature, my father was exceptionally forward-thinking and would regularly indoctrinate me with his pervading concerns on strengthening India, specifically how 'Muslims should come out of their shell and claim their rightful place;' this was his overarching passion.

If religious awareness was a profound lore of my childhood, so too was nationalistic pride bordering on jingoism, but in my case, there was no corresponding concept for other countries wherefrom my close kith and kin made me aware of the success stories of those places. Growing up, I developed a deep passion for my nation, and was very sensitive to any criticism of India. I remember the time my father's European neighbour passed a remark on an Indian child, who was begging for food at his gate. The neighbour screamed, "You Indian bastard!" to that poor, pained, defenceless boy. I remember initially feeling shocked and angered at how one human being could so callously behave towards another, and then immediately feeling a piercing sadness for where that boy would walk to next from that gate, where that boy would spend the night, and for how long he could endure this pain. Sadness then found its locale in my heart with anger towards that neighbour, spirited anger in the sentiment of using 'Indian' as an insult, as ridicule, as an abuse. As I close my eyes today, with that impression etched in my mind, I still feel those emotions as raw and unfiltered as they were at that time.

As I transitioned into young adulthood, I dreamed of finding a medium of self-expression that also contributed to the awareness of society, and I realized the natural convergence of those two desires was film. Over the course of my career, I performed in approximately fifty highly successful films as a leading actor, and as I evolved both personally and professionally, I realized I wanted to contribute to more than just entertainment; I wanted to be a messenger of social, moral, and ethical ideals.

These ideals were personified in movies such as *Chandi Sona*, which had an all-encompassing theme of compassion to those physically challenged and in need of protection, empathy, and respect; *Abdullah*, a film I'm often closely linked with, was centred on the values of communal harmony intertwined with national integration.

Assalamualaikum Watan 'May Peace Be Upon You'

These experiences organically created an embedding in my mind to always illustrate my concern about the plight of my Muslim brothers and sisters, and this triggered an endeavour to make *The Sword of Tipu Sultan*. It was my fervent ambition to ignite the minds of my Muslim brothers and sisters in creating a TV serial centred on a great Indian-Muslim hero and patriarch, who laid down his life for not surrendering to the British.

Fortunately, ambition blossomed into reality as *The Sword of Tipu Sultan* became one of the biggest successes of its time, a highly appreciated and critically acclaimed mega-serial loved and universally accepted by all communities. One of the highlights of this success was the privilege to address a large audience, as part of a political election campaign in Uttar Pradesh in 1991.

The focus of my message was to imbue the hearts of my Muslim brothers and sisters with zeal, passion, and urgency to reclaim their rightful place in their country. I remember the intensity of my voice as I stood there talking to them, trying to be heard over their fervent chants of 'Tipu Sultan Zindabaad!' At that very moment, two strands of thoughts hit my mind. Firstly, if our people could show as much zeal in their daily lives as they were showing right now, our serial, economical, and educational targets would be met and the sky would be the limit. Secondly, as an artist to remain outside the abstract world of meticulous creation and be ensconced in the spirit from the lives touched by my art was one of the greatest satisfactions and humbling moments of my life. I've always believed in the fundamental elixir of altruism. Duty and compassion became inalienable from my being, from my intent observation of my mother's characteristic of philanthropy, generosity, and warm-heartedness. I learned from her to always help people without expecting anything in return, as she always told me "Son, you're the hand of God and God is guiding to help people." I've developed that sentiment throughout my years and nowhere has that indelible belief been tested more than in the aftermath of the fire tragedy on the set of *The Sword of Tipu Sultan* that almost, and probably would have, cost me my life.

The factual aftermath of this horrendous tragedy was that fifty-two of the fifty-six crew members died; I was one of the only four survivors, after undergoing hundreds of critical operation hours interspersed across seventy-two surgeries to reconstruct the majority of myself. I was hospitalized for the next thirteen months. However, the permeating impact this traumatic experience had on my life was nothing short of sublimity. Enduring that experience spearheads and motivates my persona with every breath God has blessed me to take.

Tenacity and vision were always two of my favourite words, and two characteristics I have always strived to embody. It's at the edge of our existence that we find who we truly are, and I found out that tenacity and vision were intrinsically stitched to the fabric of my soul.

Excerpts from *The Best Mistakes of My Life*[4]

It was nine o'clock on that surreal night in Mysore; my writer and I were sitting together outside the studio having tea and discussing the next day's work, while the crew was arranging lighting inside. All of a sudden, we heard a roaring commotion and rushed through the small doors of the set.

Flames were towering over the walls, the left side of the stage completely engulfed by the inferno, and in the midst of yelling orders to help people evacuate, I was struck in the back of the head with what was later determined as a tin of exploding paint. I carried that hole in my head and focused on the job at hand of saving all of my crew. In retrospect, never could I have fathomed the severity of that crater in my head, one that would bullishly and imposingly remain for an excruciatingly painful nine months.

Amidst the frantic chaos and my own adrenaline levels shattering their limits, I didn't even initially realize the flames on my clothes burning my entire body. Impulsively feeling an intense burning, I immediately rolled over several times on the ground, remembering what to do in case of a fire catastrophe from the countless western movies I had watched. I had no idea how truly charred and burnt I was, and in that condition I rushed four of my assistants to the car and we were desperately driven to the hospital.

The car literally sped up the steps of the hospital inciting a crowded commotion of doctors, nurses and staff. As I decrepitly came out of the car with a slice of the sole of my left foot dangerously exposed, I remember the ghastly look of the hospital staff, even instinctively taking a step back at the sheer shock of my sight, before rushing to may aid as I meekly summoned the energy to say, "I'm Sanjay Khan, please help us." An assistant director who was fortunately not on the scene of the fire came rushing into the ward. I told him, "Please inform my wife that there was an accident, but please do not alarm her."

My next memory of this ordeal was waking up in an ambulance dying of the most severe thirst I'd ever craved in my life. The ambulance, amidst blocking off-street routes in real-time, was feverishly rushed to Bangalore, a distance of more than 100 kilometres. That's all I can ever recall before the pall of downy darkness descended over my mind.

I was told that February 10th, 1989, was my first of many nights in Mumbai's Jaslok Hospital. I was in a coma for two months and by the will of God, came back to life in April. The man entrusted with resurrecting me, Dr Buch, a Gujarati gentleman who had been brought by my good friend Yusuf Lakdawallah to my bedside in Bangalore, had whispered in my ears: "Mr Khan, if you stay in this hospital, you will die. I will save your life, move to Bombay (Mumbai) immediately."

He convinced my family to have me transferred to Mumbai in order to ensure the most intensive and sophisticated care for my extraordinary condition. Dr Buch was acutely concerned with my plight, so much so that while he himself was undergoing spine surgery, he made meticulous arrangement for the transfer of my oversight to Dr Narendra Pandya, another gem of a human, who continues to be one of my best friends today. I am forever indebted to these two angelic souls for saving my life.

Dr Buch spent six months in treating me with multiple surgeries, as a result, he had a severe back ailment and was hospitalized for surgery himself. As he was unable to treat me at that time, he handed the reins over to Dr Narendra Pandya, another equally capable and respected doctor. Dr Buch died some years later, may his soul rest in peace.

I am equally grateful to Dr Narendra Pandya who took over the task and then did many of the multiple surgeries on my back prior to my departure to the U.S.A. for more aggressive surgeries on my left hand. Dr Narendra Pandya accompanied me and stayed by my side for almost a month, cancelling all his appointments in Mumbai. These three gentlemen, all Hindus, were instrumental in saving my life, a Muslim. This goes to show that in our inner heart we see no difference amongst us fellow humans. My gratitude will always remain for both these noble souls.

After spending the night in delirium and extreme pain, I was aroused by the doctors. I opened my eyes to see my wife Zarine's serene presence. I was completely oblivious to my condition. I came to know later that I looked like a huge black bloated body. As I look back now, I realize the pain my wife must have gone through to see me in that condition. To this day I remember the calm, composed look of my wife, looking at me with her lustrous eyes and a faint smile. The smile triggered my energy and confidence.

I instantly told her, and smiled as I said, "Don't worry, darling, we'll start shooting in a couple of weeks." The strength of my voice gave her courage of assurance; and in turn, the strength of her eyes gave me the courage to stay alive. Along with Zarine, my brothers Feroz Khan, Shahruk, Akbar, Sameer, and sister Dilshad, who were all deeply shocked and concerned, stood in vigil around my bedside for months along with my wife and my children, Farah who was 19 at that time, Simone who was 18, Sussanne who was 13, and Zayed, the youngest at 9 years of age.

I am deeply grateful to my cousin Mirza, who drove me to Bengaluru from the site of my accident in an ambulance. Here I must also mention my close friend Ghulam Nabi Azad who was by my side and was closely monitoring the situation and reporting back to Rajiv Gandhi, who was then the Prime Minister of India.

I am indebted to Rajiv Gandhi for his support during the fire tragedy. I was later told by Ghulam Nabi Azad, that in the midst of a late-night Cabinet meeting, Rajiv Gandhi saw the news flash on Reuters about the Mysore Fire Tragedy, and I understand, he took Ghulam Nabi aside and told him: "Our friend is in trouble, help him" and immediately sent him to Bangalore with two specialist doctors. He further ordered the Government of Karnataka to rush me from Bangalore to Mumbai for better treatment. On his instructions, the roads were cleared for the ambulance and a special Indian Airlines plane with thirty seats removed to accommodate the stretcher was made available.

I had to survive a severe case of septicaemia, which is the infiltration of high amounts of bacteria in the blood and causes infections throughout the body. For weeks, I laid on specially imported rubber bed sheets, as my entire body was continuously oozing puss and blood despite bandages and initial grafts. Overcoming this condition required dozens of surgeries and 108 pints of O-positive blood. As the story of my fight was being illustrated to various media outlets, I was so deeply touched by the congregation of cadets from the Indian Army, Navy, and Air Force that selflessly queued up to donate their blood I vitally needed. Yet throughout this ordeal, I would definitely say my wife and children were far more courageous than me. I remember my children, Farah, Simone, Sussanne, Zayed, had to retake a year of school as they missed their April final exams, being in the midst of this trauma.

To see a loved one suffer is a far more piercing pain; the pain of a loving spectator is so much more consuming than the pain of a sufferer. Yet I was so impressed with my three daughters and son in how they unswervingly rallied around their mother, displaying unconditional responsibility, depth, and love. I was most proud of my children's courage and grace under pressure and I continue to admire them today; I thank Allah every day for blessing me with such a treasure of a family.

In the hospital, I encountered a strange illusionary experience, as I myself didn't know the magnitude of the crisis I was in. Besides my family and brothers and sister, the ruling elite of Delhi, including stars of screen and forces of industry, would continuously come to visit and shower me with pathetic, sad, and pitied looks. I'll never forget Dharmendra, one of the top Bollywood actors of that time, crying like a baby and telling me with a tone of deafening despair, "Don't worry, Brother, I'm with you." I later realized all my well-wishers were briefed that I wouldn't last long and every time a visitor graced me, I would be consumed by the same eerie feeling of witnessing my own funeral from the vantage point of my burial. In my solitary moments, isolated with only my consciousness, thoughts, and vulnerabilities, I truly wasn't sure if I would survive.

My case became so hopeless that I felt like a small insect trapped within a huge vertical greased cylinder, relentlessly attempting to grip a side of that slippery surface, in the desperate hope to eventually climb out from the top. But that insect's attempts, with every slip and fall, felt like an exercise of imposing futility. All I wanted to do was fly out of this cylinder like a bird and join humanity once again. With restrained wonder and yearning, I imagined the simple treasured interactions of life; a conversation with my entire family around the dining table, the joyous exchanges of pure laughter with friends, creatively brainstorming with collaborators on an artistic pursuit.

I was always grateful to Allah for my life, but I now fully embraced the appreciation for each momentary thread connecting life's experiences. The agonizing moments have caused strange convulsions and reminded me of Mirza Ghalib.

One morning during my seventh month of hospitalization, just before my departure to the United States for more aggressive treatment, I was watching television in my room when, suddenly and inexplicably, everything became blurry. I had just lost my sight and my immediate reflex was one of panic. Instinctively my mind raced to ask, "Is this the end?"

But after three or four thunderous heartbeats, I calmed down, reached for my nurse, and said, "Nurse Roxane, I think I can't see." She immediately rushed me onto a stretcher and our odyssey from the seventeenth to the first floor of the hospital truly appeared like eternity. As I was lying on the stretcher and being frantically rolled to my specialist, my mind couldn't shake the relentless and pounding notion that I could endure the most extreme physical pain, but I couldn't lose my sight; that's an adversity too steep and profound to overcome. Thankfully, Dr BK Shroff, the eye specialist, said my retina was intact and my eyesight would return as I regained my strength. However, for the next several days, I didn't tell anyone of this additional impairment, as I didn't want to further burden my wife and family with increased franticness.

I delicately shared the experience with my wife only after a couple of days, to spare her the anguish. With this apprehensive reality just between the two of us, I quietly took my prescribed vitamins and after a few weeks, they brought me back my sight for a brave and beauteous world.

Just before my relocation to the United States for the next phase of my attempted restoration, Nurse Roxane was given a daunting task: breaking the news to me that the fire resulted in the death of all but four individuals. As she uttered each syllable, I was exponentially more stunned, shocked, and poignant. I had just automatically assumed everyone else was recovering in the hospital rooms, guided by the specialists and regimented by the medications. This was the moment the surreal barricaded the way into the real. Alone, I cried inconsolably that night in my hospital room, their faces streaming into my mind, drowning my consciousness. The magnitude of that tragedy persisted within me for several months, and I carry the scars of that wound with me every day.

After my initial eight months at Jaslok Hospital in Mumbai, I was transferred to Georgetown University Hospital in the United States for intense grafting and rehabilitation. The men architecting and overseeing this multi-layered process—Dr Scott Spear and Chief Orthopaedist Dr Bogamal—first had to examine my completely mangled left hand. I was given two choices: either be implanted with a perfectly configured artificially cosmetic hand but one with extremely limited functionality, essentially a glorified showpiece of a hand; or be subjected to surgery attempting to unlock and declaw my real hand for actual use. The hand wouldn't look ideal but, if surgically performed successfully, would allow me to drive, write, and golf. After careful pondering and despite the risk, I opted for the latter without serious trepidation, but implicit faith in God all the same.

My surgery was scheduled for a cold and cloudy February morning in 1990, and my anxiousness had evolved into an acute depression. As I was being rolled onto the lift to go to my surgery theatre, I was grindingly and wearily fighting the thoughts of my lost splendour. But as I entered the lift, I unequivocally believe that I received a sign from God. At that moment to my right was an African American woman with both arms and both legs amputated. I saw the dense shade, of the dark rings under her eyes, had that surrendered inward look as if looking into the past. I remember choking up and almost shedding a tear when I was surged by the epiphany that I still had my hands and feet that I wasn't in that dire a condition, that things could be so much worse.

Armed with this refreshed vigour, I went into the surgery theatre with a full heart and thirteen hours later, had the successful outcome Allah had destined me for. Today, whenever I golf, drive, write, or even pick up a bag with my left hand, I always think of Dr Spear and Dr Bogamal. Their presence, warmth, and implicit factual explanations gave me immeasurable comfort. I will forever be grateful to the United States for their ingenuity and always be impressed with the kindness and concern of the American medical community. Yet, it was my visceral belief in that sign from God that nourished me with the resolve to ultimately be called 'Miracle Man' by Dr Spear and Dr Bogamal.

I was truly the one in a billion case, as never in medical history had a person at the age of forty-seven survived from sixty-five per cent third-degree burns. I never lost my faith in my Allah, and it was this faith in my God, courage in my heart, and the passion to complete *The Sword of Tipu Sultan* that kept me alive to strive, to seek, to find, and not yield.

However, even after all my surgeries and the single-minded determination that relentlessly consumed me to conquer, my circumstance wasn't always susceptible to the natural ebbs and flows of apprehension and uncertainty. I was devastated to see my face after many months and wondered in my moments of intense pensiveness if I could ever face the cameras again. My wife urged me to fulfil my promise to my people of playing the role of Tipu, as the initial nineteen episodes brought a plethora of expectations from millions of fans that I simply could not give a go by.

On being finally discharged from the hospital after this enduring battle for my survival, I wanted, as a professional and for the best interest of the serial, to also provide a face and dialogue test to Shabaaz, who was playing the role of Hyder Ali, in order to determine if he would be a more compelling Tipu. Yet on-screen, it was evident that I was evoking and personifying the tragic character of Tipu quite seamlessly and I took that as a sign from God that I was destined to complete the series by doing the role. When I returned on set, I was so frail that I couldn't sit on the horse by myself. There was an air of mystery and wonder if I reasonably had the physical endurance and capability to do justice to the role so inexplicably intertwined to my destiny.

The true test presented itself on a hot June afternoon. Zarine was sitting by my side as my stunt double was prepared to act out a scene involving a battle between Tipu Sultan's army versus the British Cavalry. All eyes were fixed on Tipu's favourite white horse, and as the scene was about to commence, a burning thought refused to leave my mind: *Today, if I don't take the shot myself, I'll be running like a white rabbit, helter-skelter destination unknown.* Come what may, even with my left hand deeply incapacitated, I held the reins of the horse with that very left hand and tightly squeezed the sword with my right. I couldn't feel my left leg, as it was fifty per cent numb; my wife was very reluctant to allow me to do this but she saw the need in my face to exercise my fears and conquer the depths of my demons. We exchanged looks, and with a tone of loving resignation, she said, "Please be careful."

The crew delicately helped me mount on the horse and I went to the point of the charge with terrified exhilaration emanating through my entire body. There were two hundred cavalry horses with riders behind me from the 61st Cavalry of Rajasthan, carrying with them drawn swords and lances. As I seemingly caressed the flesh of my insecurities, I kept telling myself: *There's no way I can fall or I'll get pierced by a sword and lancer.* As the cue for action was only a few precious moments away, I took the name of Allah, believed firmly in his will, and surrendered everything in his hands. It was Allah's inspiration that allowed me to complete the charge, but my personal tour de force was only beginning. The horse got even faster after passing the camera, and unable to control the horse with my left hand, I had to drop my sword on the ground. Fearing that a carelessly flung sword will injure the riders following me, I leaned down on my saddle so that I could toss the sword flat on the ground. Quickly regaining my position, I controlled the horse with both my hands just in the nick of time and preventing it from jumping into a thick thorny babool bush. The crew erupted in a roaring standing ovation as I looked at my wife with a proud mischievousness.

Unbeknownst to all, however, was the fact that I was bleeding profusely from my left hand and leg. So, I subtly snuck off to the make-up room, quickly changed my clothes and cleaned myself off. I returned back to the set, quietly sat down, took a smooth reflective breath and smiled . . . that was the day I came back to life. It was an exponential recovery in self-esteem after that day and I returned from the depths of my despair, better than ever. *The Sword of Tipu Sultan* was completed with rousing adulation.

This huge fire calamity did not slow me down but generated enthusiasm and energy to do more work. I plunged into my work and created three more mega-series: *The Great Maratha*, *Jai Hanuman*, and *1857 First War of Independence*. I subsequently reinvented myself as an ambassador of entrepreneurship by conceptualizing and building one of the most beautiful luxury deluxe five-star hotels in India—The Golden Palm Hotel and Spa in Bangalore.

Later, my passion for Indian history and love for our culture gave birth to an idea to create and construct a grand

Assalamualaikum Watan 'May Peace Be Upon You'

theme park under the brand name of '7 Cities Theme Park & Themed Entertainment Destination', a unique best-in-class theme park to celebrate five thousand years of India's colourful and rich history, civilization, and culture, for which we were invited by the Government of Gujrat when Shri Narendra Modi was the chief minister. We struck off very well right with from the first hand shake, and he welcomed my team which included architect Hafeez Contractor, Sunil Alagh, and Anirban Dutta Gupta, the creative director, with warmth. Honourable Narendra Bhai was so impressed with our audio visual presentation of the 7 Cities Theme Park, he requested us to repeat the screening once again. Visibly excited and interested, he went on to express in no uncertain words: "This is a dream, I would be happy to give you land to choose from six important locations, including Sardar Sarovar and Dhulera, and will clear the project immediately."

He expounded his dream about the huge plans he had for the new capital city of Dhulera. He wished to construct a huge dam connecting both sides of the Bay of Khambhat with an eight-lane superhighway and rail tracks for rapid action transport mobility, cutting the distances and time of travel between two sides of the Bay. The landward side of the Bay would receive and store the sweet waters of the seven rivers of Gujrat into this gigantic reservoir instead of letting it flow wastefully into the sea. On the banks of Dhulera, he expressed his intention to plan the 21st century capital smart city of Gujrat with worldwide connectivity. As he explained this to me I could see the force of his determination in his eyes. In the course of our conversation, he also mentioned the plans he had for making the Statue of Unity, honouring the great Sardar Patel, and even showed me a drawing of the statue to be constructed. I looked at it carefully and said, "If you don't mind, may I make a comment?" He instantly said, "Please do." I simply mentioned, "Sardar Patel's statue is looking tired, he should have more resolve in the posture" Narendrabhai quickly looked to his right, where his OSD Kalyan Nathan was seated and said, "Kalyan Nathan, did I not tell you the same thing that Sanjayji is saying?" Kalyan Nathan nodded.

Looking at the Sardar statue today, standing tall and proud, I cannot help but believe that the Dhulera dream of the honourable Prime Minister will also soon be realized.

I found him to be very cordial and a scintillating conversationalist, charming and charismatic. Our meeting time with him was meant to be for fifteen minutes, but it extended beyond an hour. At the end of the meeting, honourable Narendra Bhai gave me a big hug and mentioned, "On my next visit to Mumbai I will give you a call."

My next meeting with Narendra Bhai was in the lobby of The Great Maratha Hotel where he was being ushered by his security for Hema Malini's daughter's wedding. Walking right behind me and my family with his security, I quickly turned, when I realized it was him and greeted him. Narendra Bhai met us warmly, and after the exchange of pleasantries, asked me why I did not come back for the project. Considering where we were, I tried to make it as short as possible and literally whispered in his ears, "I will come and explain after you become the prime minister."

Our plans to build 7 Cities in Gujrat were distracted by the churn of politics due to the then coming general elections of 2014.

The extraordinary mandate he received in the 2019 Lok Sabha elections indicates the people's allegiance in his leadership. The first five years of his regime were quite eventful, specially so the dynamic turn in uplifting India's image internationally was a superbly designed craftmanship of charm diplomacy and personal reach out bringing India new respect and recognition. However, I reserve my comment on demonetization, but GST implementation with few amendments keeping in view the future of India has long term benefit to the country.

I will not join his critics by saying nothing was achieved during his first term. I will only describe it as a foundation laying ceremony for the present tenure to fructify and stabilise the country towards long-term redressal of problems, starting from the poorest in this country and reaching out to all deserving sections of the society and making India into a land of peace prosperity and growth not only economically but also socially with benevolence amongst its people, as only a united country can exhume strength to meet the challenges of the coming times including climate change and water shortages. It's a prodigious challenge for him to keep India on course—a country of twenty-nine states with an aspirational population of 1.35 billion multi-lingual, multi-cultural, and multi-religious people who are eagerly looking up to his leadership with great expectations and hope for their redemption from hunger, joblessness, health, farmer distress, below the line poverty, and the uncertainties of day-to-day challenges for survival.

I have faith in our Honourable Prime Minister to keep his commitment of 'Sabka Saath Sabka Vikas Sabka Vishwas' and lead the nation in the pursuit of happiness, social justice and equality.

While on one hand, I had my entrepreneurial dreams, on the other, my thoughts were always occupied by the Muslim position in India and how I could inspire them with my example and assist them in gaining their rightful place in the society. I wish that the young men and women of today keep this story in their psyche and carry it with them in their day-to-day lives as an example of embracing challenges and recognizing the invincibility of truth. Truth conquers all and is an indestructible and invincible phenomenon, an elixir for life's victories.

As the transcendent poet, philosopher, and politician, Muhammad Iqbal said: *'When truth has no burning, then it is philosophy, when it gets burning from the heart, it becomes poetry.'*

If truth is on your side, you are invincible, and the absolute truth is Allah. I resolved myself into this truth despite losing my eyesight, my hair (which eventually grew back), and shrivelled to a teenager's weight, and today I stand as the personification of the miracle.

After going through this experience, I'd often look up where the skies blend with space, searching for God and for truth. The beauty of the believer's life is in being infused by the supernatural when trying to rationalize the might of the natural. That infusion was a sense that God purposefully preserved me to do something good, yet the tangibility of that good was still unknown.

In the process of the creation of this book, it dawned upon me that I needed to make an indelible difference in the lives of my people. Therefore, I have resolved to dedicate the remainder of my time on this earth in creating a revolutionary Indian-Muslim Socio-Economic Trust (IMSET), an entity that I have continuously and iteratively conceptualized over the course of the past few years. This organization, independent of any political party and devoid of government's empty philosophical rhetoric, will be entrusted to redeem and re-establish respect within the Indian-Muslim community by providing tangible services, valuable resources, and developmental opportunities in the areas of education, IT technology, banking, health, sports, industry, agriculture, social service, medicine, arts, and law for ambitious Indian-Muslims of all ages. I want to dedicate the entirety of my thoughts, efforts, and desires to witness my fellow Indian-Muslim brethren regain status and potential in their lives and discover their rightful place in the sun of accomplishment and strengthen India with all their might.

The IMSET will transform apathy into action, transpose existing mentality with rational outlook, and transcend all claustrophobic obstacles and be carried forward on a continual basis.

The underlying essence of this organization will be the proliferation of educational excellence that will organically translate into professional achievement. I want my fellow brothers and sisters to remember that the unprecedented and ubiquitous wave of Islam's spread was achieved by the ilm (i.e. learning) of Prophet Muhammad, rather than by the sword.

Remember, the Quran is a message to inspire from and aspire to; it's one's inspiration to be educated and inspire others. As Fazl-Ur-Rehman, author of *Major Themes of the Quran*, has eloquently synopsized: 'It must be constantly remembered that the Quran is not just descriptive but is primarily prescriptive. Both the content of its message and the power of the form in which it is conveyed are designed not so much to 'inform' men in any ordinary sense of the word as to change their character. The psychological impact and the moral import of its statements, therefore, have a primary role.'

The seed of Islam's mission has always tightly interlocked hands with education, as the annals of history have revealed. Madrasas being the first educational centres providing university-level training in commerce, philosophy, science, and mathematics. At its intrinsic essence, education is fundamentally the disciplined acquisition of empiricism and rationality.

As such, Muhammad Iqbal profoundly stated: 'From a study of the Islamic religion it would become clear that it is a rationalistic religion and as shown by our Prophet Muhammad its formulae could be practical in everyday life. By contrast, the philosophy of ancient Greece could not make much headway in metaphysics. Greek philosophers believed in mysticism—the obscure and the abstract. But Islam teaches that one should believe only in what is rational and empirical.'

My personal view is that for today's Muslim India to unconditionally embrace the fruits of education, we must eradicate the penumbra of fear that has continued to intoxicatingly overwhelm us for a long time. This fear has gathered momentum due to a government system that has neglected our youth and failed our citizens, without the proper sustenance for success. We must break the shackles of this fear and resignation, and constructively exercise our frustration by putting our minds to work and start learning. Fear is to be removed from the mind the way impossible is to be removed from the dictionary.

As the age-old proverb states, a journey of a thousand miles starts with a single step. The journey is upon us now, it's time to say Assalamualaikum to this journey and use the concept of the IMSET as its roadmap, its guide, and its compass. No matter how long, adverse, or daunting a journey, I want to fervently push the IMSET to the heights of its potential and to the centre of the mainstream. Let's embark on this adventure of reclamation together, and in order to reclaim, we must revive, and in order to revive, we must revisit our knowledge base with all its accretions and avoid vacuous adherence to stereotypes. Knowledge as embellishment is snarky and the same knowledge, when seen in the right perspective, becomes our unrelenting friend.

Through all the minutes, hours, days, months, and years of my life I have gained strength from this simple message: carry truth, always, in your hearts, as it is invincible, indestructible . . . it will speak for itself.

Today I share it with you all.

SECTION II

THE SAGA OF HINDUSTAN

As filmmakers, we are the true magicians of time. We can stretch it or condense it, slow it down or speed it up, bring it forward or send it back. But when I try to look back at the history of this magnificent land, I realize that I will need considerably more dexterity and skill to compress the glorious chapters of Indian history and culture into a few short sentences.

Known from time immemorial as the land across the Indus, or 'India', this magical land and its five millennia of interweaving stories can only be told slowly, lovingly, and with a great deal of patience. But I will still try and trace, in a highly condensed form, the history of India and its people.

Romain Rolland wrote, 'If there is one place on the face of earth where all the dreams of living men have found a home from the very earliest days when man began the dream of existence, it is India.'

Perhaps no nation on earth has had so profound an influence on world history as India. Modern genetic research has positively identified groups of individuals closely related to the earliest humans who had originated in Africa. Tracing back the recurrence of the C-M130 gene in the Kala tribal population in modern-day Kerala, it has been proven that humans entered and settled in the Indian landmass about 70000 years ago.

While early humans in the Northern hemisphere were still eking a living by scavenging for food from caves, advanced civilization, based on trade and commerce, was flourishing in the river valleys of the Indus. The prosperity of its time could be sensed from the fact that copious amounts of energy and money were spent on activities that enhanced the quality of life. The roads were paved, the cities had sewage system, advanced architecture, wells for freshwater, granaries, ports for transcontinental trade, and large buildings with public amenities. The fact that it did not have a standing army reveals that it was a centre so essential to all other tribes and communities around that their own survival was intrinsically linked to the safety and continuity of the Indus Valley Civilization. Our root, if we can trace it, is from the people of these times.

The decline of this extraordinary civilization, one of the greatest of the river valley civilizations and definitely the most advanced—the others being on the banks of Nile, Euphrates, and Tigris, and the Yellow River—was the change in weather, probably due to heavy deforestation combined with an extended period of drought. The civilization, fragmented and desperate groups, migrated further inland which coincided with the arrival of migratory tribes from the steppes of Central Asia—the Aryans. While many historians paint this period as a replacement of the old Indus civilization with the new Aryan invasion, I believe it was a slow amalgamation of both the cultures. The Aryans integrated the animalistic and elemental worship of the old—Rudra became 'Lord Shiva'—into their pantheon of gods, to name just one of the many examples. This is the true magic of India where the outsider, the invader, and the guest became the citizen, the defender, and the host. They came to India to conquer but got conquered instead. Over the years waves of invaders have come, only to be amalgamated within the crucible of this nation, to emerge wiser and stronger.

India's history and culture is dynamic, spanning back to the beginning of human civilization. It begins with a mysterious culture along the Indus river and in farming communities in the southern lands of India and is punctuated by constant integration of migrating people with the diverse cultures that surrounded the land. Available evidence suggests that the use of iron, copper, and other metals was widely prevalent in the Indian sub-continent from a fairly early period, which is indicative of the progress that this part of the world had made. By the end of the fourth millennium BC, India had emerged as a region of highly developed civilization.

The history of India begins with the birth of the Indus Valley Civilization, more precisely known as Harappan

Civilization. It flourished around 2,500 BC in the western part of South Asia, what today forms Pakistan and Western India. The Indus Valley was home to the largest of the four ancient urban civilizations of Egypt, Mesopotamia, India, and China. Nothing was known about this civilization till the 1920s, until the Archaeological Department of India carried out excavations in the Indus valley wherein the ruins of the two old cities, viz. Mohenjo-Daro and Harappa were unearthed. These ruins showed that these were magnificent merchant cities—well planned, scientifically laid, and well looked after. They had wide roads and a well-developed drainage system. The houses were made of baked bricks and had two or more storeys.

The highly civilized Harappans knew the art of growing cereals, and wheat and barley constituted their staple food. They consumed vegetables and fruits and ate mutton, pork, and eggs as well. Evidences also show that they wore cotton as well as woollen garments. By 1500 BC, the Harappan culture came to an end. Among various causes ascribed to the decay of Indus Valley Civilization are the recurrent floods and other natural causes like earthquake, etc.

Then came the Vedic Civilization, the earliest civilization in the history of ancient India. It is named after the Vedas, the early literature of the Hindu people. The Vedic Civilization flourished along the river Saraswathi, in a region that now consists of the modern Indian states of Haryana and Punjab. Vedic is synonymous with Hinduism, which is another name for religious and spiritual thought that has evolved from the Vedas. The Ramayana and Mahabharata were the two great epics of this period.

India's greatness has been defined by cohesion and not by fragmentation. The greatest achievements in art, culture, science, and technology occurred when India and various fractious fighting feudal kingdoms were bought under a strong central administration. But it also set the stage for periods of greatness that hoisted India to the epitome of economic and cultural power. The Mauryan empire under Ashoka ruled over the entire Indian subcontinent and was the force behind the spread of Buddhism all over the world; the Gupta empire is known as the golden age of Indian civilization with probably the greatest outpouring of Indian inventions and genius; the Chola empire of peninsular India spread the greatness of India far beyond its shores through active trading and maritime policies as far as Indonesia; the Delhi Sultanates followed by the Mughals with its ultimate amalgamation of Islamic philosophy with the Hindu way of life finally unified the nation.

Prior to the Muslim advent, after the fall of the great Hindus and Buddhist empires, (650CE Chalukya ruler Vikramaditya 1 to 98CE Cholas in the South, Northern India broke up in many several small kingdoms) India was a continent of disparate principalities and inverse people. The history of Muslim rule in India goes back to later Ghaznavids (977 to 1186CE) who ruled from Lahore after shifting their capital from Ghazni. Founded by Sabuktigin, it rose to prominence under his son Mahmud of Ghazni.

The annexation of Punjab by the Ghaznavids unlocked the gates for further incursions. After the second battle of Tarain in 1192 AD, India came under the Muslim rule and the Delhi Sultanate in 1206 AD inaugurated a new era of variegated hues in Indian history which lasted for almost 650 years.

Historian Harbans Mukhia, an authority on medieval India, describes colonization as 'governance of a land and its people, now on behalf of and primarily for the economic benefits of a community of people inhabiting a far-off land.' According to him, the Mughals came to India as conquerors but lived in the subcontinent as Indians, not as colonizers. They merged their identity as well as that of their group with India and the two became inseparable, giving rise to an enduring culture and history. He goes on to say Mughals being seen as foreigners was never a point of discussion till quite recently, so well had they integrated and assimilated into the country they had made their own. There was no reason for it either, since Akbar onwards, all Mughals were born in India with many having Rajput mothers and their 'Indianness' was complete.[5]

Babur had invaded India at the behest of Daulat Khan Lodi and won the kingdom of Delhi by defeating the forces of Ibrahim Khan Lodi at Panipat in 1526 AD. Thus, he laid the foundation of the Mughal empire and commended his future generations to come with an impassioned message eloquently captured in his Baburnama:

'Son, this nation Hindustan has different religions. Thank Allah for giving us this kingdom. We should remove all the differences from

our heart and do justice to each community according to its customs. Avoid cow slaughter to win over the hearts of the people of this land and to incorporate the people in matters of administration. Do not damage the places of worship and temples which fall in the boundaries of our rule. Evolve a method of ruling whereby all the people of the kingdom are happy with the king and the king is happy with the people. Islam can progress by noble deeds and not by terror. Ignore the differences between Shia and Sunni as this is the weakness of Islam. Keep the people following different customs integrated into a single whole so that no part of the body of this kingdom becomes diseased.'

Most Mughals contracted marriage alliances with Indian rulers, especially Rajputs. They appointed them to high posts, with the Kachwaha Rajputs of Amber normally holding the highest military posts in the Mughal army. Emperor Akbar followed the policy of Sulh-i-Kul meaning universal peace.

It was this sense of a shared identity with the Mughal rulers that led the Indian sepoys who rose up in 1857 against the British East India Company in the first war of Indian Independence, to turn towards the aged, frail, and powerless Mughal Emperor Bahadur Shah Zafar—they crowned him Emperor of Hindustan and decided to fight under his banner. Between the 16th and 18th centuries, the Mughal empire was the richest and most powerful kingdom in the world and as French traveller, Francois Bernier, who came to India in the 17th century, wrote, 'Gold and silver come from every quarter of the globe to Hindustan.'

This is hardly surprising considering that Sher Shah and the Mughals had encouraged trade by developing roads, river transport, sea routes, ports, and abolishing many inland tolls and taxes. Indian handicrafts were developed. There was a thriving export trade in manufactured goods such as cotton cloth, spices, Indigo, woollen and silk cloth, salt, etc. Indian merchants trading on their own terms and taking only bullion as payment led Sir Thomas Roe to say, 'Europe bleedeth to enrich Asia.'

I have often admired the origins of the elegant and exquisite arts and crafts, the pashmina shawls, the handicrafts, carpets, textile weaving of Kashmir, which led me to discover the contributions of Sayyed Ali Hamadani who travelled widely—it is said he traversed the known world from East to West three times. In 774 AH/1372 AD Hamadani lived in Kashmir. After Sharaf-ud-Din Abdul Rehman Bulbul Shah, he was the second important Muslim to visit the region. Hamadani went to Mecca, and returned to Kashmir in 781/1379, stayed for two and a half years, and then went to Turkistan by way of Ladakh. He returned to Kashmir for the third time in 785/1383 and left because of ill health. Hamadani is regarded as having brought various crafts and industries from Iran into Kashmir; it is said that he brought with him seven hundred followers, including some weavers of carpets and shawls, who taught the craft of pashmina textile and carpet-making to the local population. Ladakh, likewise, benefited from his interest in textile weaving. The growth of the textile industry in Kashmir increased its demand for fine wool, which in turn meant that Kashmiri Muslim groups settled in Ladakh, bringing with them crafts such as minting and writing.

This trade was traditionally in the hands of the Hindu merchant class. In fact, Bernier wrote that Hindus possessed 'almost exclusively the trade and wealth of the country.' Muslims, on the other hand, mainly held high administrative and military posts. A very efficient system of administration set up by Akbar facilitated an environment of trade and commerce. This led the East India Company to seek trade concessions from the Mughal empire and eventually control and destroy it.

A very interesting painting, in the possession of the British Library, named *The East Offering Her Riches to Britannia*, dated 1778, shows Britannia looking down on a kneeling India who is offering her crown encrusted with rubies and pearls. The advent of the famous drain of wealth from India started with the East India Company, not the Delhi Sultanate or the Mughals. Edmund Burke was the first to use the phrase in the 1780s when he said, India had been 'radically and irretrievably ruined' through the Company's 'continual drain' of wealth.

Let us examine India's economic status prior to its becoming a British colony.

The Cambridge historian Angus Maddison writes in his book, *Contours of the World Economy, 1-2030 AD: Essays in Macro-Economic History*, that while India had the largest economy till 1000 AD (with a GDP share of 28.9% in 1000 AD) there was no economic growth. It was during the 1000-1500 AD that India began to see an economic growth with its highest (20.9% GDP growth rate) being under the Mughals.[6]

By 1700, under Aurangzeb, Mughal India had become the world's largest economy, ahead of Qing China and Western Europe, containing approximately 24.2% of the world's population and producing about a quarter of the world's output. Mughal India produced about 25% of global industrial output into the early 18th century. India's GDP growth increased under the Mughal empire, exceeding growth in the prior 1,500 years. The Mughals were responsible for building an extensive road system, creating a uniform currency, and the unification of the country. The Mughals adopted and standardized the rupee currency introduced by Sur Emperor Sher Shah Suri. The Mughals minted tens of millions of coins, with the purity of at least 96%, without debasement until the 1720s. The empire met global demand for Indian agricultural and industrial products.

Cities and towns boomed under the Mughal empire, which had a relatively high degree of urbanization (15% of its population lived in urban centres), more urban than Europe at the time and British India in the 19th century. Multiple cities had a population between a quarter-million and half million people, while some including Agra (in Agra Subah) hosted up to 800,000 people and Dhaka (in Bengal Subah) with over 1 million. Of the total workforce, 64% were in the primary sector (including agriculture), while 36% were in the secondary and tertiary sectors. The workforce had a higher percentage in non-primary sectors than Europe at the time; in 1700, 65-90% of Europe's workforce was in agriculture, and in 1750, 65-75% were in agriculture.

In the 18th century at the time of Emperor Aurangzeb, India had overtaken China as the largest economy in the world.[7]

In 1952, India's GDP was 3.8%. "Indeed, at the beginning of the 20th century, 'the brightest jewel in the British Crown' was the poorest country in the world in terms of per capita income," said ex-Prime Minister Manmohan Singh. In 2016, on a PPP-adjusted basis, India's was 7.2% of the world GDP.

Since it's established now that the Mughals did not take away money, let's talk of what they invested in. They invested in infrastructure, industries, factories known as karkhanas, in building great monuments which are a local and tourist draw, generating crores of rupees annually. As per figures given by the ministry of culture in Lok Sabha, just the Taj Mahal built by Shah Jahan has an average annual ticket sale of more than INR 21 crore. (There was a drop in visitors to the Taj Mahal in 2018 and figures stood at INR 17.80 crore.) The Qutub Complex generates more than INR 10 crore in ticket sales, while Red Fort and Humayun's Tomb generate around INR 6 crore each.[8]

A beautiful new style known as Indo-Islamic architecture that imbibed the best of both sensibilities was born. The Mughals invested in local arts and crafts, and encouraged old and created new skill sets in India. As Swapna Liddle, the convenor of INTACH's Delhi Chapter says, "To my mind, the greatest Mughal contribution to India was in the form of patronage to the arts. Whether it was building, artisanal crafts like weaving and metalworking, or fine arts like painting, they set standards of taste and perfection that became an example for others to follow, and brought India the global recognition for high-quality handmade goods that it still enjoys."

Mughal paintings, jewels, arts and crafts are the key possessions of many a western museum and gallery as they were looted in and after 1857. Some can be found in Indian museums too.

Art and literature flourished under the Mughal empire. While the original work was being produced in the local and court languages, translation from the Sanskrit to the Persian, too, was taking place. Akbar also encouraged the translation of the Ramayana titled Ramayana-I-Masihi and the Mahabharata titled Raznmana to dispel the ignorance that often led to communal hatred. Akbar, for the first time, established Darul Tarjuma (Department of Translation at Fathepur Sikri) in order to know more about the Hindu religion. Sumer Chand, who translated the Ramayana from the Sanskrit to the Persian in 1715, started the Ramayana with 'Bismillah al-Rahman al-Rahim' (In the name of God). Emperor Akbar himself arranged for the book illustrations of the Ramayana and the Mahabharata.

Dara Shikoh's Persian translation of the Upanishads, named Sirre-e-Akbar, was taken by Bernier to France, where it reached Anquetil Duperron, who translated it into French and Latin. The Latin version then reached the German philosopher, Schopenhauer, who was greatly influenced by it and called the Persian Upanishad 'the solace of his life'. This awakened an interest in Post-Vedic Sanskrit literature among the European Orientalists.

It wasn't only Mughal emperors who were building structures—Hindu mansabdars and traders were building temples and dharmshalas in many cities, like Vrindavan, Mathura, and Banaras. Maharaja Surajmal Jat and Raja Nahar Singh built Jama Mosques in Bharatpur and Ballabhgarh. Madhuri Desai, in her extremely well-researched book *Banaras Reconstructed*, writes: 'The riverfront Ghats bear an uncanny resemblance to the Mughal fortress-palaces that line the Jamuna river in Agra and Delhi.'

It's dangerous to generalize history, especially on communal lines. While economic deprivation for the ordinary Indian existed, as it did in other societies of the world, but as Frances W. Pritchett, Professor Emerita, Columbia University, says, 'The impression one gains from looking at social conditions during the Mughal period is of a society moving towards integration of its manifold political regions, social systems, and cultural inheritances. The greatness of the Mughals consisted in part at least in the fact that the influence of their court and government permeated society, giving it a new measure of harmony.'

The number of Hindus employed by the emperor's administration in Mughal history is the highest during Aurangzeb's reign. Under Aurangzeb's reign, Hindus rose to represent 33.6% of Mughal nobility, the highest in the Mughal era. This was largely due to a substantial influx of Marathas, who played a key role in his successful Deccan campaign. During his time, the number of Hindu

Mansabdars increased from 22% to over 31% in the Mughal administration, as he trusted them to continue his fight in the Deccan.

The Mughal system of revenue and taxation was sophisticated, involving collectors, assessors, and paper managers. This is what made the Mughals wealthy and powerful. The successor kingdoms of the 18th century inherited these traditions and modified them, in places such as Bengal, Awadh, and the Maratha territories.

The British quickly moved to employ former Hindu scribes and paper managers who had served the Mughals and their successor states. These penmen came primarily from a Hindu caste called Kayasth, and they provided the company with valuable rent rolls, records of past assessments, and the paper, factual sanction to enact revenue demands.

Thus, to say that the Mughals looted India is a falsification of history. Since it's established now that the Mughals did not take away the wealth of India, let's talk of what they invested in. They invested in infrastructure, industries, factories known as karkhanas.

The Mughals have been an immutable part of India's history, adding to its rich fabric with their talent and valour. To wish for a past or a present and a future sans them is being imprudent.

The other great contributor to the development and growth of India was the great Tipu Sultan, the king of Mysore.

Tipu Sultan was the first ruler in India to establish

the first Chamber of Commerce in Mysore. Along with this, it has been mentioned in the history of banking that Tipu Sultan introduced modern banking methodology and encouraged exports to earn foreign exchange, thereby increasing the general wealth of the population and the gross domestic product of the State. Tipu Sultan was not just a brilliant strategist but he also had sound economic sense. His enterprises across Mysore and the rest of the world included factories in Kutch, Muscat, Karachi, Mahe, Pune, and Nagore.

All this was looked after by a corporation instituted by him. The main purpose of the corporation was trade. It had to buy at reasonable rates locally and export them through its factories. In a very interesting order, Tipu asked the officials of his corporation to raise capital from the public as well as through inviting deposits. These were to be held on an annual basis with the principle to be returned after a year along with the interest earned. The interest was termed 'nafa' (profit).

We also have with us the interest rates on each deposit, which varied with the size of each deposit, smaller depositors earning more interest.

A deposit of 5-500 Imamis (Silver Rupee, 10.7-11.6 gms.) received 50% interest. A deposit of 500-5000 Imamis (Silver Rupee, 10.7-11.6 gms.) received 25% interest. A deposit of over 5000 Imamis (Silver Rupee, 10.7-11.6 gms.) received 12% interest.

Tipu Sultan wanted to encourage weaker and the less affluent to invest their savings with his corporation. In those days most of the money was hoarded at home or buried around somewhere. He was pragmatic enough to move away from a core Islamic concept of Interest-Free loans. This shows his farsightedness. Today almost all Islamic countries have interest levying banks in the garb of profit sharing.

Among other things, he had established many centres for animal husbandry, to improve the quality of horses and bullocks. He imported horses from Persia and Arabia which were brought by his merchant fleet to improve the breeding stock of the State. The Kunigal Stud Farm, started by him, still exists today. He brought bulls from Kathiawar in Gujarat to improve the local breed, which were hardier and could move heavier loads at a faster clip and it doubled up as beasts of burden tilling the land to improve the productivity of the crops and to move his heavy artillery during military campaigns. The 18th century ruler—who was the last hurdle to the British's domination over South India—introduced ground-breaking changes to the economy and even created technology parks across his kingdom.

Till this date Karnataka earns immense amount of foreign exchange by way of silk export and employs 7.9 million people. The silk industry was mentored by Tipu Sultan who sent delegations to China to gain the technology and know-how for producing silk of the greatest quality. He supported this endeavour by import of silkworms to establish the silk industry.

With examples such as Tipu Sultan, it is worrisome to

notice the lack of entrepreneurial skill and business talents amongst the Indian Muslim community. Not only was he far-sighted economically, his understanding and respect for the environment was also well known. Once when he was visiting the River Cauvery, he saw dead fishes floating in the water. On enquiry he was told that it was due to the discharged effluent from a nearby gunpowder factory. He issued an immediate 'farman' (order) to shift the factory stating that god has created the flora and fauna for man's survival and that if they were wiped away then the human race would become extinct. He also created canals linking his lakes and reservoirs as well as keeping original run-off channels free of encroachment and construction which fed the Cauvery. These were provisions for times of calamity—for excess water to run off in case of floods and allow water to flow in case of droughts. This becomes extremely relevant in today's world wherein our headlong rush towards industrialization and urbanization we are consistently ignoring the environment and the very earth that feeds us. The recurring floods in many parts of India are just some of the few examples of man-made disasters that are affecting us.

The numerous letters ransacked from Tipu's library were confiscated; the Wilkes brothers were present at the time of the fall of Seringapatam in 1799, May 4th, as part of the East India Company army as mentioned in Alexander Beatson's book on the siege and fall of Seringapatam published in 1800. The Wilkes brothers' experts in Persian language translations claimed that they had discovered several correspondences of Tipu Sultan ordering the killings of Hindus and carrying out forcible conversions and destruction of Hindu temples. These forged letters were ostensibly mixed in with the confiscated correspondence and made public surreptitiously. Obviously, the politics behind this has gone viral to this day in disparaging the name of this great ruler.[9] Several Kannada folk songs (lavanis) lamenting his death were in circulation in the 19th century, the earliest dating back to 1800, the year after he died in the battlefield. This is a very special fact since folk songs do not exist for any of the kings of Karnataka. They exist for only tragic heroes like Tipu Sultan and other local chieftains who died at the hands of the British.

It's not difficult to see how people of diverse faiths and regions have come together and stitched the fabric of India. It's always best to read history backed by facts, based on documented evidence written and accepted by world-renowned historians and researchers, and not WhatsApp forwards, where people often share false information to suit their own bias. It will only be fair to warn the future generations of the effect the absence of a factual and fascinating history of this great land will have if it is hidden and reconstructed to benefit an ideology. It will deprive them of this wealth of knowledge. Real history has an uncanny knack of emerging from the labyrinths of the earth and playing havoc when it does.

DIVIDE AND RULE

As *The Rough Guide to India* puts it: 'It is impossible not to be astonished by India. Nowhere on Earth does humanity present itself in such a dizzying, creative burst of cultures and religions, races and tongues. Enriched by successive waves of migration and marauders from distant lands, every one of them left an indelible imprint, which was absorbed into the Indian way of life. Every aspect of the country presents itself on a massive, exaggerated scale, worthy in comparison only to the superlative mountains that overshadow it. It is this variety that provides a breath-taking ensemble for experiences that is uniquely Indian. Perhaps the only thing more difficult than to be indifferent to India would be to describe or understand India completely. There are perhaps very few nations in the world with the enormous variety that India has to offer. Modern-day India represents the largest democracy in the world with a seamless picture of unity in diversity unparalleled anywhere else.'[10]

By definition within the Constitution of India, I belong to the minority community. However, I have reservations about this definition. I have always considered myself to be Indian and at the same time a person of my faith, a Muslim. I love my country as much as my religion. I love my religion as much as my country. My earliest world view—regards for all and respect for the law of the land— was set by my father. It never occurred to me to see myself and my interaction with the rest of the society through the narrow prism of my religion alone. I believe we should do away with the terminology 'minority' altogether. To me it automatically denotes a community which is 'inferior' and needs 'help' to become equal to the 'majority'. Our pro-active intervention should be based on economic needs regardless of which community one comes from. The entire spectrum of Indian society should be reviewed and the Government of India should take the initiative to aid. People of various faiths should be officially addressed as Indians, and if the question arises, then as Indian-Hindus, Indian-Muslims, Indian-Christians, and so forth. This will bring forward a sense of pride amongst all citizens who will identify themselves first as Indians and then as a person of their faith.

Any medium that has mass appeal is prone to be misused for personal gain. And so the same has happened with religion, which on many occasions has been turned into a tool for political action. A society depends on functioning as a unit, each individual supporting the larger welfare through own individual contributions. If not for altruistic purposes, for the pragmatic functioning of the state, the community, and the individual peace is necessary. The common man on the street does not want enmity with his neighbour as they are dependent on each other. Therefore, the clash of religion—Hindus vs Muslims, Christianity vs Islam, for example—is a myth created by those who seek to maintain a position of strength, for who wants a strong nation when it is easier to rule a chaotic broken country? We have seen these cards of play from the beginning of time—the stories of Shakuni from the epic Mahabharata, to Kautilya's Arthashastra and also the colonial Divide and Rule policy.[11]

But we are more mixed and more similar than we are made to believe. Not only are we sons and daughters of the same soil, we also come from the same roots. Majority of the Muslims in India are rebels against the ingrained casteism of the prevalent order of those times. Gradually the new and young religions of Christianity and Islam, brought in through the traders and the explorers, the merchants and the invaders, questioned the core doctrines of the Vedic-based religions—that you are born into your caste and therefore you cannot aspire beyond the set boundary as defined by the caste. Therefore, a Sudra will always remain a Sudra. The new religions questioned this: you may be born a Sudra but you are equal in the eyes of the Almighty. For many, it was a way out from the cycle of rebirth and restraint.

India's greatness has always been defined by its cohesion than by the purported fragmentation. Because how can a country where the language, the food, the dress, and the culture change every few hundred miles exist as anything but a cohesive coherent state? This is the greatness of India—the tolerance for differing thoughts and respect for others' way of life. Many have tried to drive a wedge between these and all have failed. Those who have embraced it have excelled. Four great religions of the world have emerged from this milieu: Hinduism, Buddhism, Jainism, Sikhism, and it has embraced four others: Islam, Christianity, Judaism, and Zoroastrianism. It is told that when the first Parsis landed in modern-day Gujarat, escaping persecution from Persia, the local ruler sent a glass covered to the brim with milk—implying that the land had no place for the visitors. In return the Parsis sent it back after mixing sugar in it—the message being that we will mix seamlessly with you and like how sugar sweetens the milk, we will enrich your life. Similarly, everyone who has set foot in this country has added their bit of the sweetness—some more than the others, some out of necessity, and some through intentional integration into the society.

Seventy years after India gained its Independence from British colonial rule and suffered the pain of the Partition, the nation struggles to define its soul. India's politics today is about which party wins the majority in the legislature, whereas it should be about defining the personality of this modern nation. It's about who is India and what is

India. It's a struggle to define the narrative of this nation informed by its true history and not by any mythological constructions that deviate from what India is.

Mahatma Gandhi, the Father of the Nation, drew the attention of the entire world by achieving freedom through passive resistance, also known as Satyagraha, without firing a single bullet. This formidable and unique movement was first of a kind in the annals of history, which has been recognized by the world as one of the greatest moral re-armament of a nation.

Inspired by the pristine message of Gandhi, Martin Luther King's Civil Rights Movement pulverized America and helped the emancipation of the American 'negro' to break the shackles of fear and tyranny and paved the way for the Black American to seek his rightful place in his country. Nelson Mandela too followed the peaceful teachings of the Mahatma. He suffered twenty-seven years of imprisonment but in the end freed his people. Both these leaders drew their inspiration from the Mahatma giving India the recognition as the moral authority of the world.

The British recognizing the power of the Indian people and its vast resources, devised a treacherous policy of Divide and Rule not only between Hindus and Muslims but went as far as dividing the society into ten sub-castes to conquer and subjugate this proud civilization and kept them stripped of their dignity, wealth and honour, under the British boot for almost two hundred years. The evil machinations and ploys adapted by them were to disparage and damage the images of the great Muslim kings of India whose contributions throughout the centuries—not only in its robust growth but also protection of the country against the incessant Mongol invasions—are indeed immense and immeasurable in a factual sense. Thereby the British commissioned Sir Jadunath Sarkar to write voluminous distorted work on Alamgir Aurangzeb, the clairvoyant Emperor who made India not only the cynosure of the world but also the richest country.

The reason I have ventured to present selected portions defining periods of Indian history is to ignite thought and to let the readers draw their own conclusion instead of learning and believing in the rhetoric of the right-wing groups who in their lust for power are blind to the larger picture.

The historical section of work has been drawn from some of the greatest researchers, scholars, and historians from India and the world to testify its authenticity and give you a true view of the facts which are eloquently and logically expressed. The readers will find the information exciting and satisfying, providing a sense of history in my message on the need of the Indian-Muslim to pursue education.

To look at the position of Muslims in today's India and the Hindu Muslim ethos, we have to go back to the colonial history of India.

History is a discipline, which links the past with the present and the present forms the basis of the future. History is concerned with handing of tradition and lessons of the past into the future, so no age, no country can do away with history. Research in medieval Indian history has changed from theme to theme over the last two hundred years. However, we have still not been able to change the mind-set of the present and till today medieval age is at times referred to as 'Dark Age' in which no development took place and is often equated with anarchy and barbarism.

The past has not been understood as a process and instead we have had characters around whom history has been constructed. So, we know Akbar and Aurangzeb, Shivaji and Maharana Pratap, Muhamad Ghazni and Jaichand as nodal points around whom the idea of nationalism, secularism, liberalism, fanaticism, and treachery have been woven. And this is how, also, the narrative of a Hindu ruler becoming the form of an expression of nationalism was drafted by the East India Company.

Another impression created was the development of two monolithic communities in medieval India whose sole preoccupation seems to have been to fight each other. This idea was first developed by James Miller, which gave rise to the periodization of Indian history as that of Hindu, Muslim, and British periods. It crystallized the concept of a uniform, monolithic Hindu community dominating early history as did the Muslims equivalent in the subsequent period with relations between the two becoming conflicted. In today's circumstances, it becomes even more so contextual when Somnath is linked with Bamiyeh and Taliban is perceived as Islam.

A glimpse into official British records will show how this policy of Divide-et-Impera was taking shape. The Secretary of State Wood in a letter to Lord Elgin [Governor General Canada (1847-54) and India (1862-63)] said: 'We have maintained our power in India by playing off one part against the other and we must continue to do so. Do all you can, therefore to prevent all having a common feeling.'

George Francis Hamilton, Secretary of State of India, wrote to Lord Curzon: 'I think the real danger to our rule in India not now, but say fifty years hence is the gradual adoption and extension of Western ideas of agitation, organization and if we could break educated Indians into two sections holding widely different views, we should, by such a division, strengthen our position against the subtle and continuous attack which the spread of education must make upon our system of government. We should so plan educational text-books that the differences between community and community are further strengthened.'

Foreign travellers provide great insight into the Mughals, but scholars have often privileged European works above Indian sources without cause and failed to appreciate how western historians have spun fantasy and reality together. Sir Jadunath Sarkar's extensive work commissioned by the British with an ulterior motive is a fine example of this misdeed. In his extensive work on Aurangzeb, his anecdotes are a tempting text with lots of juicy titbits and contains misinformation with detailed illogical episodes. He was a self-made historian who made the most substantial contributions to scholarship on Aurangzeb in the 20th century. He translated several Aurangzeb period histories and a collection of letters into English and published numerous books on Aurangzeb, including the five-volume *History Of Aurangzeb*. For a long while, Sarkar had the last word on Aurangzeb but my analysis of his contribution to Aurangzeb is that it was overly communal and lacked historical rigour. The following chapter will unfold many of these facts and myths created by the Raj.[12]

The last Mughal emperor, Bahadur Shah Zafar, led the War of Independence in 1857 in alliance with Nana Saheb, the unfortunate last Peshwa of the Maratha empire, Maulvi Azimullah Khan, Tatya Tope, Begum Hazrat Mahal, and Rani Laxmibai of Jhansi and numerous other courageous patriotic Indian both Hindus and Muslims. A country-wide war was to begin simultaneously on the 31st of May 1857, but the Indians in the British army revolted before that on the 10th of May 1857.

A startling 5,00,000 Muslims were martyred following the events of 1857, of which 5000 were Ulema (religious scholars). It is said that there was not a single tree on the Grand Trunk Road from Delhi to Calcutta where a limb or body was not found hanging for days together.

Indian Ulema called for Jihad against the British and declared India as Darul Harb (Territory under Enemy control). This call found resonance all over the country with Muslims rising up against the British. To liberate the countrymen from the cultural and educational bondages of the colonial empire, towering centres of learning like the Darul Uloom Deoband, Darul Uloom Nadwa, and the Aligarh Muslim University were established in the late 19th century, which are still counted amongst the leading Indian seminaries.

The Reshmi Rumaal Tehreeq was launched in 1905 by Shaikhul Islam Maulana Mehmood Hasan and Maulana Ubaidullah Sindhi to unite all the Indian states against the British. Maulana Mehmood was imprisoned in Malta and Kalapani for the same where he breathed his last!

There are 95,300 freedom fighters names written on India Gate, Delhi, out of that 61,945 are Muslim names, which means 65% freedom fighters are Muslims.

The Indian National Congress, from the time of its inception to independence, has seen nine presidents who were Muslims!

Barrister MK Gandhi served in a law firm in South Africa owned by a Muslim, who on his own expenses brought Gandhiji to India in 1916. Here, he started his agitation under the Ali Brothers.

The Mopla movement in Kerala, saw 3000 Muslims being martyred in a single battle.

The Non-cooperation Movement and the Swadeshi Movement saw overwhelming Muslim participation. Janab Sabu Siddiq who was the Sugar King of that time gave up his business as a form of boycott. The Khoja and Memon communities owned the biggest business houses of that time and they parted with their treasured industries to support the boycott.

The 1942 Quit India Movement was actually planned

by Maulana Abul Kalam Azad. He was imprisoned on the 8th of August and sent to Ahmednagar, because of which Gandhiji had to lead the movement on the 9th of August.

Jyotiba Phule was sponsored by his neighbour, Usman Bagban, in his educational activities, so much so that the school in which he taught was owned by Mr Usman. His daughter, Fatima, was the first girl student there and joined as a teacher thereafter!

Muslim leaders always supported the Dalit cause. In the Round Table Conference held in London, Maulana Muhammad Ali Johar was lured into abandoning the Dalit cause in lieu of accepting all the other demands of the Muslims. But Maulana Johar refused to forsake the Dalits!

When Dr BR Ambedkar could not win the 1946 central elections, the Bengal Muslim League vacated one of its own seats and offered it to Dr Ambedkar, who won it in the by-poll. This gesture by the Muslim League paved the way for his entry into the Constituent Assembly and the rest, as they say, is history.

Muslims freedom fighters were active in the field of journalism as well. Maulana Azad used his pen against the British despite being prevented by the colonial powers a number of times. In fact, the first journalist to be martyred in the cause of India's freedom struggle was also a Muslim—Maulana Baqar Ali.

The classic and most brutal example of using religion as a tool of division was perfected by the British through their 'Divide and Rule' Policy. While conflicts between Hindus and Muslims have existed, it was not 'commercialized' as it was under the British. If the hatred between the Hindus and Muslims were as severe as we have been made to believe, then in the more than 650 years of Muslim rule in India, not a single temple would have been left standing and probably the entire population would have been converted to Islam. If one is to believe that it was spread by the sword; it is entirely not logical to convert millions and millions. Islam is a religion of equality of mankind, which was a rare social order of those days.

Throughout the ages, from the dawn of time, the rich and the mighty kings and emperors ruled selfishly, destroying life and liberty, oppression of the weak in a society which was divided by them at their mere whim. This brutal, cruel, and oppressive order survived for centuries. The birth of Islam with its appeal of equality and fairness was absorbed by millions of people across the globe for its egalitarian spirit and appeal. Hence, the rapid Islam-ization of the world from the Arabian heartlands to the furthest corners of the globe. Therefore, it would not be correct to say that Islam was spread by the sword, the conquest of the oppressed lands by the Arab Muslims invasions is normally understood as the sword mis-termed.

Quite often it is alleged that Indian society is 'highly stratified', 'disintegrated', and 'discriminatory'. It was not so all the time. Rift has been purposely encouraged and created within the society for political purposes. One such example that highlights this false impression exists even today.

In the small village of Khera Sadhan, with a population

barely touching 10000 and only 50 kilometres from Agra, it is common even today to have a family which is half Hindu and half Muslim. Here they worship in temples and dargahs, Eid and Diwali are both celebrated with equal fervour. Shabana, a college student who hails from Khera Sadhan, reflects this ideology: "Our philosophy of life is to live and let live. People must be free to worship God in whatever form they like." There are many examples like Khera Sadhan where people from the spectrum of India believe in commonality and freedom of expression. However, attempts are constantly being made and have been made to bring down this wall of tolerance. The colonial divide and rule is one such example and probably the most effective and scientific in its approach and implementation.

India was a great centre of attraction for the British empire. For British rulers, India symbolized Imperial grandeur. They believed that Britain's superpower status for most of the nineteenth century and some of the twentieth depended on their control over India and its vast resources. Viceroy Lord Curzon had expressed it clearly in 1901 when he said: 'As long as we rule India, we are the greatest power in the world. If we lose it we shall drop straightway to a third-rate power.' Quite early, the British realized that as long as they adroitly exploited the religious, linguistic, and historical divisions that marked Indian society they were relatively safe.[13]

The British colonial rulers had a clear aim and objective in mind—that of total control of the land and its resources. They saw the population as a means of labour, a market for goods and at worse, rabble of the worst kind—to be discarded and side-lined if required. To achieve this objective with only a handful of officers and bureaucrats, they had to find a way to weaken the society from inside, gnaw away at the foundations. They adopted and adapted the divide and rule theories, inflamed the differences that already existed in the society and adroitly established their empire in India by playing off one part against the other.

In order to justify their domination and imperial rule in India, British propagated theories of racial superiority, of 'White-race', and the so-called 'White Man's Burden'. They rewrote history, propagating the 'Aryan Invasion Theory', which promoted the idea that Caucasian Aryans from the central steppes of Europe came down into the fertile valleys of the Indus and took over from the Indus Valley Civilizations. It was these Aryans who brought in knowledge and prosperity. This made the 'white' British rule more 'acceptable' to the Indians, as it created a false sense of linkage and common ancestry. Modern research has proved that this is not true. While the Aryans did come, it was more of a trickle and not a deluge, and a great degree of amalgamation did take place between the original inhabitants of the Indian subcontinent and the newly arrived Aryan herders.

Building upon these series of orchestrated disinformation campaigns, the British rulers, missionaries, philosophers, writers, and historians vehemently denounced the culture, character, and social structure of the 'native' people. This destroyed the confidence and mental strength of many educated Indians so deeply that they considered native practices indefensible.

Literally overnight, in historical terms, we Indians became third-class citizens. Till the 17th century, India and China were the largest economies in the world. By the end of the 19th century, we had been relegated as the begging bowl of the world. In the late 19th century and 20th century, famines killed more Indians than any other man-made disasters. It is only now, as we slowly dismantle the two centuries of misrule, that we are again regaining our position in the world order.

The colonialists launched an ideological attack on the citizens, specially targeting the educated Indians in their effort to secure a reasonable combination of various races and castes in administration and other industrialized sectors. British rulers were well aware that they had managed to retain an empire in India by taking advantage of the diversities of Indian people and by playing them against one another—princes against people; Hindus against Muslims; castes against castes; and provinces against kingdoms.

The 1857 uprising changed everything. The uprising by Indian sepoys, supported by various princely states, is now considered to be India's first war of Independence, resulting in the British East India Company being replaced and India being brought under the direct rule of the crown. The fact that soldiers came from all castes and communities and were united under the nationalistic banner, fought shoulder to shoulder like brothers—forgetting their caste and creed, fighting for a nation, a common future—shook the British. They realized how tentative their hold over India was. A united India, with a gentle shrug, could topple them. An aggressive policy was required that permanently drove a wedge between the shallow divisions of the society, creating wounds so deep that they would not heal easily.

Immediately after 1857 the British adopted a policy of 'Apparent Association', which lasted till 1905. The purpose was to keep the 'natives' busy with their internal problems so the ruling elite and the business interest could continue without any distraction. The common plan of action was: '. . . we must continue to do so. Do what you can, therefore, to prevent all having a common feeling.'

After the martial law post 1857, the massacre of entire sections of Indian society—ostensibly as 'an emotional reaction to the massacre of the English'—the colonialists, now firmly entrenched in India, started dismantling the social structure and oversaw the disintegration of the Indian society through three carefully stage-managed steps—by appeasing the Hindus, then the Muslims, and lastly, they devoted their attention to backward castes.

Initially, the British, who annexed authority from the Mughal rulers, looked favourably towards the Hindu community. The Hindus were encouraged to opt for modern education. It was a logistical problem. Just not enough English officers were available or willing to come to India for a subordinate or lower posts in administration. Secondly, as the British had annexed the administrative authority from the Mughals, who were Muslims, it was assumed that the Hindus would be natural partners after more than 650 years of Mughal and Muslim rule.

In Macaulay's *Minutes on Indian Education* it is succinctly noted: 'The colonialists saw the middle classes' growing influence and their hold on the Indian intelligentsia and community as a potential threat to their rule in India. They considered it necessary to counter this by raising a strong force against them. The British encouraged the formation of many caste groups to counter the dominance of the Hindu middle class in administrative services. They allowed other communities to form political groups on the basis of caste and community. The movement against the perceived 'advantageous groups' forged ahead with ferocity in the southern and western parts of India.'

In the name of equality before the law and providing equal opportunities, certain sections of society were given 'preferences' on the basis of caste and financial assistance and preferences in education and government employment at local and provincial level were provided. Quotas were assigned for government and other administrative jobs for non-Brahmins, Muslims, and Anglo-Indians with the objective of ostensibly opening the doors of new opportunities of advancement and progress to other castes and communities, who hitherto had been denied the same. It served the purpose of creating new rifts and tensions by selective preferential treatment. While this did help many of the community members who otherwise would not have had the opportunities to rise above societal dictated position, the practice of preference was indulged in a selective and highly preferential manner, not necessarily based on broad-based indicators or benchmarks like economic position, etc. This created a section of the community who was indebted to the British and would, therefore, be loath to go against them, and secondly fanned the flames of communal fire by open discrimination.

In parallel to this, the British played on the Muslims' grudge over the loss of their dominant political position. The seed of fear of being dominated by the majority Hindu community was sown around this time and fervently nurtured. During the 1850s, Mohammedan Anglo-Oriental College was established at Aligarh. English principals like Archibold, Theodore Beck, and Morrison played an important role in keeping Muslims away from mainstream thought and inculcating in them a feeling of separation.

In 1920 it was renamed as Aligarh Muslim University. Sir WH Gregory, while appreciating the Resolution of Government of India on Muslim education, wrote to Lord Dufferin, the British Viceroy in India, in February 1886: 'I am confident, that it will bear good fruits, indeed, it seems to have done so already by the complete abstention of the Mohammedan from Brahmins and Baboo agitation. It will be a great matter to sweeten our relations with this portion of the Indian population, the bravest and at one time the most dangerous.'

In 1885, Eutice J Kitts, the British Ambassador to Azamgardh, listed, for the first time, backward castes and tribes based on the 1881 Census. The objective was to give them financial assistance and preferences in education and government employment. This exercise is of importance as this was the first time that the government officially recognized caste as a base for the purpose of governance.

Initially special schools were opened for those listed, for those seen as requiring 'preferential' education. Various tools were used to encourage education including special scholarship, loan, hostel facilities, and concessions in school fees. In 1885, the education department proposed to reserve 50% of free scholarships for backwards and Muslims, as scholarships purely on merit grounds would perpetuate middle-class Hindu monopoly. The follow up to these reservations was a reservation in administrative position to ostensibly provide opportunity to those from the backward classes and Muslim community.

These seeds of communalism through selective preferences which were sown earlier blossomed during Lord Lytton's Viceroyalty (1876-80). On October 1st, 1896, a deputation of Muslims led by His Highness Sir Agha Khan put forth the demand of a separate electorate. Seizing this opportunity, on December 30th, 1906, a separate party, cajoled and instigated by the British—the Muslim League—was launched to pursue and safeguard Muslim interests. The other pan-Indian party—the Indian National Congress—had a clear charter of being representative of both the Hindus and the Muslims, including safeguarding all communities' religious and cultural beliefs.

Therefore, the Muslim Leagues' sudden demand for

a political representation only along the line of religion was one more pawn in the political chess game that had become India. The creation of the Muslim League and the acceptance of separate representation for Muslims were enshrined in the Minto-Morley Reforms and in effect became the first effective constitutional route of communalization of Indian politics. The Minto-Morley Reforms known as Government of India Act of 1909 devised a novel method to distribute and balance the power between Hindus and Muslims.

The introduction of modern education, initially seen as a way of educating the 'natives' to the 'modern European' way of thinking was soon usurped to create a cabal of English literate semi-educated 'native Indian' lower-level administrative officers. It was necessity and not nobleness of thought that compelled the introduction of large scale 'modern education'. Initially the Indians were excluded by the British colonialists from every honour, dignity, or office. But the geographical and logistical difficulty of shipping a large enough workforce to man such a massive country made it imperative that an increasing number of subordinate or lower posts in administration be filled by locally educated Indians.

However, even the education system was shrewdly used as a tool for imperial designs. The intention of introducing modern education was, as Lord Macaulay said: 'To form a class, who may be interpreters between us and millions of whom, we govern, a class of persons, Indian in blood and colour, but English in taste, in opinion, in morals and in intellect.' It was mainly to get Indians 'anglicised in terms of both cultural and intellectual attainment.'

The unintended side effect was that the key to the treasures of scientific and democratic thought of modern West was suddenly available to the highly intelligent Indians. It opened up the doors of knowledge and widened the mental horizons. In due course of time, it produced many scientists, national leaders, and reformers who used the system to beat the system.

In the near absence of industrial, commercial, or social service activity, the educated Indians depended entirely on government jobs. This led to a keen competition between different sections of Indian society. But education is a double-edged sword—it not only produced many mediocre government servants to fill the lower levels of administration, but also, by the second half of the 19th century, many national leaders of extremely robust intellect, like Dadabhai Naoroji, Ferozeshah Mehta, Gokhale, Mahatma Gandhi, Jinnah, Bal Gangadhar Tilak, Lala Lajpat Rai, Moti Lal Nehru, Jawahar Lal Nehru, Subhash Chandra Bose, Maulana Abdul Kalam Azad, Sardar Vallabhbhai Patel and many more. This was an unwanted side effect.

The Policy of Reservation was yet another tool that was used to fan the embers of communal discrimination. In 1918, the Mysore Government appointed the Miller Committee to look into the question. On its recommendation, 'all communities, other than Brahmins, who were not adequately represented in the public Service' were declared 'backwards'. In 1921, preferential recruitment for backward communities was instituted formally for the first time in colleges and state services.

The concessions bestowed on the backward communities made them loyal to British rule. An excerpt from the *Times* archives of August 1925, shows that in the fifth non-Brahmin Conference in Tanjore, Rao Bahadur O Thanikachalam Chetty of Madras, 'warned the non-Brahmin public of the dangers ahead' and how in the name of Swaraj, deception was being practised, lies were being broadcast with a view to creating prejudice against the Justice party, and to secure transfer of power to Brahmins under the guise of supporting the Swarajis.

This organization, along with numerous others, were supported and encouraged by the British colonialists. A parallel can be seen in today's time where a multitude of Non-Government Organizations (NGO) have mushroomed with the backing of foreign financial assistance to act as pressure groups with specific anti-national objectives. Census operations were also used for the purpose of further splitting the communities by creating political identities in India. Census operation, the introduction of electoral politics, and suggestion of the Census Commission for 1911 Census, to exclude untouchables, (comprising about 24% of Hindu population and 16% of the total population in 1908) from Hinduism, had made position of untouchables or Harijans prominent in Indian political scene.[14]

Mahatma Gandhi along with other national leaders regarded it as the 'unkindest cut of all, which would create a permanent split in Hindu society, perpetuate casteism, and make impossible the assimilation of untouchables in the mainstream.' Dr Rajendra Prasad said, 'The electorate in 1919 was broken up into ten parts, now it is fragmented into seventeen unequal bits . . . giving separate representations to Schedule Castes further weakened the Indian community. Division on the basis of religion, occupation, and service was made. The British introduced every possible cross-division.' Lal Bahadur Shastri denounced the whole happenings 'as a shameless episode of the national history of the country.'

The Indian politicians inherited from British rulers four powerful weapons i.e. electoral policy, an archaic bureaucracy which was designed to run an empire deliberate and slow, census operations, and reservation policy to perpetuate class divisions for the sake of vote-bank politics. I am astonished to this day as to why the founding fathers of our nation did not take remedial measures to revamp the bureaucracy by striking down these very processes which have suppressed the rights of the Indian nation for over two centuries. The present trend of giving continued importance to diversities along caste, community, region, language by almost all political parties and by shrewd politicians for electoral purposes is at its peak. Instead of the feeling of fraternity amongst Indians, 'feeling of others' or 'we' and 'them' has become more pronounced. Caste, religion, regional, ideological intolerance has generated communal violence and animosities amongst its own people in the country.

If we choose the path of communal violence and internal strife, we are not far away from making a spectacle of this ancient civilization in the eyes of the world. This poisonous seed of Divide and Rule is growing. This is the most powerful and evil legacy left behind by the British which is weakening our country from within. Unchecked, this will lead to the balkanization of this great country. We, as citizens committed by our bounden duty, must not allow this rot to creep in under any circumstances.

The reader should not carry an aversion within himself and judge the present generation of the British people as arch-villains. They should not be punished for the sins of their forefathers. History must always be consistent and carried forth from generation to generation as it happened.

SECTION III

THE FLIGHT OF THE FLOCK

The story of Islam in India is as old as the story of Islam itself. Islam found its mark in India in the early 6th century when Cheraman Perumal, a Sudra king of Kerala, willingly embraced it. He had a dream where he saw the moon being split into two parts. A group of travelling Arab merchants interpreted the dream as the miracle of the Prophet. This prompted him to visit the Prophet Muhammad in Mecca, where he embraced Islam and changed his name to Tajuddin. The first mosque in India, the Cheraman Jama Masjid, was built in 629 AD in Methela, Kerala, by Malik Bin Dinar, Cheraman's companion and friend.

India, today, consists of one of the largest Muslim populations in the world after Indonesia and Pakistan. After the Partition, a large number of Muslims (especially from North India) moved to Pakistan, yet in 1951, according to the first Census after independence, there were 35.4 million Muslims living in India, which formed the largest 'minority'. Today, the Muslims of India make up 14.2% of the country's population of over 1.35 billion. Though it's such a significant number, Muslims were and still are confronted with different types of violence and face various forms of discrimination in every walk of life.

India's Muslim communities tend to be more urban than rural. In many towns and cities in northern India, Muslims are one-third or more of the population. The largest concentrations of Muslims, about 16.82%, live in the states of Bihar, West Bengal, and Uttar Pradesh, according to the country's present census.

The main grievance of the Indian-Muslim has been discrimination, especially in the economic field, with the result that they are economically worse off than the majority community. This discrimination in areas of employment, permits, contracts, and admissions to various institutes has firmly kept them out of the mainstream and in certain cases brought them to the verge of economic ruin. The Indian Constitution claims to provide equality of opportunity to all individuals, organizations, and social groups. But the biggest Indian minority is a victim of deprivation.

Whether it is legislative assemblies' educational institutions, government jobs, the problem of security in case of riots, representation in political organizations, posts in policy planning, and decision-making groups or other pressure groups, there is an acute shortage of

Muslim representation everywhere, resulting in constant social tension and problems in governance.

Communal turbulence against Muslims is among the biggest tragedies of our independent, secular democracy. Regardless of any government being in power the communal incidents are escalating. The following statistics as per the Ministry of Home Affairs India give us an in-depth view of this heinous crime.

Year	No. of reported cases
2010	701
2011	580
2012	668
2013	171
2014	644
2015	751
2016	703
2017-18	822

Communal turbulence against Muslims: Statistics as per the Ministry of Home Affairs India

I am of the view that the Modi government, which is well settled with large numbers in both houses of the Parliament, has a clear mandate to implement strong impregnable legislation to stop this carnage. These unfortunate alarming incidents must be controlled in the larger long-term interest of the nation, for peace, prosperity, and development protecting the fair image of India as world's largest democracy and a secular republic.[15] Wherever Muslims have acquired a relatively better economic position, these riots have sent them back to the starting point. The above-mentioned statistics evidences these facts. Senior Indian journalist Khushwant Singh noted that in all communal violence that has taken place in India since Independence in the 1940s, over 75% of the causalities—in terms of lives and property destroyed—were Muslim.

The rewriting of history has been done in a way that it continues to fuel the non-secular, chauvinistic right-wing Hindu perspectives, causing the new generation of Indians to shape their behaviour towards minorities in a very hostile way.

The bludgeoning population of this vast nation warrants we take serious cognizance of this exploding population issue. The planning by the government goes astray as it can never meet the target due to the extra population influx each year, year on year. The averments of Prime Minister Narendra Modi, from his 2019 Independence Day speech, to restrict growth in each family across demography to two children per family makes sense but when you get down to the brass tacks the political parties will not agree to this and will take advantage during elections to leverage voters, describing this as an evil not allowed by any religion as they say a child is a gift of god and those who assail it are radically opposed to religion. The brute majority the Modi government enjoys currently can easily be deployed to invite all political parties to sign a magna carta agreeing to the principal of two children per family only. This will automatically prevent the political parties to abstain from using this as their Brahmastra. This will also prevent the WhatsApp university scholars from spreading vile and horrid rumours that Muslims with their four wives are producing dozens of children, which eventually will push them into minority status. Any intelligent man can describe this as an unwarranted lunacy and a deliberate attempt to disturb the waters.

Then there is the economic problem: More than 50% of Muslims are leading a life below the poverty line as compared to 35% of Hindus who live below it. Because of a general environment of hostility against Muslims, decent employment in the private sector is becoming increasingly difficult for them, while in the public sector there is no encouragement either. The future of Muslim professionals and its working class, traders, etc., has been very greatly affected.

Today very few Muslims are found in government jobs. A recent survey shows that there are only eight Muslim police chiefs in India's 591 districts. That is .01% as compared to 14.2% of the Muslim population in India. The situation of other departments is also worsening day by day.

Education: The active discrimination Muslims face in the private and public sector of the job market has forced them to pay less attention to school education which, in

India, is connected with the job market. In the educational field, therefore, Muslims are very backwards.[16]

Urdu language: Another major problem of Muslims of India is that of the Urdu language. The Urdu language was born as a result of the interaction and cohesion of different languages, nations, cultures, and civilizations and is a mixture of some old languages like Sanskrit, Arabic, Persian, Turkish, etc. Urdu is almost a dead language now as far as the medium of instruction is concerned. It is not tolerated even in the primary and secondary stages of education.

The real journey of education in general and higher education in India started after 1947. Education is its journey can't stand alone but institutional roles need to be included to assess the contribution as a whole.

The institutions of higher learning are considered the most important agency of social change, social transformation, and the entire development of the country. Muslim education has always been a serious issue despite availability of so many academic institutions in general and minority institutions in particular. The poor condition of the Muslims' education can't be attributed to the government only, but the society, home, economy, motivation, employment, and similar factors.

Prospects of Muslim Education[17]

The new policy of education appeared in 2019 with the Modi government announcing INR 5 crore for scholarships to the minority students, which I consider to be miniscule. It will hardly impact the large numbers of deserving students. However, it has been felt that all the policies on education, namely 1968, 1986, and 1992, were conscious of the education and problems of minorities in this country, but nothing significant was done.

The National Policy on Education (1968) in 'Post-Independent India—Issues, Factors and Prospects' envisaged that the educational institutions run by minorities had a special place in the national system of education. The documents further stated that the administration at the centre and in the states should not only respect the rights of minorities but also help to promote their educational interests.

The Draft National Policy on Education 1979 envisaged that the institution run by religious and linguistic minorities could help in achieving the goal of an integrated Indian community. While the National Policy on Education 1986 further gave importance to minorities, saying that greater attention would be paid to the education of these groups in the interests of equality and social justice. This included a constitutional guarantee to them to establish and administer their own educational institutions and protection to their languages and culture simultaneously objectively will be reflected in the preparations of textbook and in all schools' activities and all possible measures will be taken to promote an integration based on appreciation of common national goals and ideals, in conformity with the core curriculum.

The government says it is committed to address the existing backwardness in the education of minorities, especially the Muslims. Therefore, schemes like the Prime Minister's 15-point program inter-alia aimed to enhance opportunists for education of minorities, ensure an equitable share in economic activities and employment.

This is what's missing in our Indian-Muslims of today; our community isn't a tangible configuration of resources, avenues and support, rather it's an abstract conceptualization subjected to a multitude of diverging opinions. Why can't we, the 172 million Muslims of India, create organically powerful machinery of a community? We certainly have so many successful individual Muslims to engage from; industry giants such as Azim Premji and Yusuf Humid, as well as entertainment moguls such as the Khan conglomerate in Bollywood and many more from the other fields of business, industry, and services. I am deeply concerned with the outlook of our people and the role they can play in making India the land of peace, plenty, and prosperity.

I witness on a day-to-day basis the greatest hijack of promises made and broken to Muslims by successive governments over the years, and our population is languishing under the burden of these false promises. I want to ignite the desire and passion in the Indian Muslim youth to come forward and be the emblematic faces of tomorrow's industry titans by joining the mainstream India. The only way for this utopian dream to be a reality is by stimulating the current and next generation to the promising outcomes of our own new and self-conceptualized infrastructural design.

As I perch from the ivory tower of my mind, I don't see one India progressing, rather I witness the independent matriculations of several Indias. Of all these wonderfully chaotic and energetically networked worlds, it's Muslim India that's crawling crippled in the dungeons. Let's switch on the lights.

As Prophet Muhammad has inscribed:

'Smiling even to a stranger is an act of charity. So is joining good and forbidding evil, giving direction to the lost traveller, aiding the blind, and removing obstacles from the path.'

The all-inclusive progress made by India fills me with ecstasy; what teases me out of this thought is the squalor and pusillanimity that doggedly pursue the Muslims. For this it would be appropriate to remember Prophet Muhammad for his dedication and courage for the deliverance of the message of Islam against overwhelming odds to his people.

'If you are for your community, in turn, your community is for you.'

If you take a look at India's most successful ethnic communities, such as the Parsi, Bohra, Khoja, Sikh, Buddhist, and Jain, you'll realize there is a convergent pattern of behaviour in mentality. Parsis are regarded as an institutional community integral to the economic and historical development of India with icons such as Jamsetji Tata, known as the 'Father of Indian Industry', as well as members of the Tata, Godrej, and Wadia industrial families.

According to the 2001 census, they only consist of

approximately 70,000 individuals in a land of 1.2 billion. Furthermore, Parsis have the highest literacy rate (97.9%) of any Indian community (India's national average rests at 64.8%). Not coincidentally, Parsis are the epitome of philanthropy and citizenry as they have established sophisticated grassroots social security infrastructure through their panchayat system. The core fund of this system is known as the Anjuman or community chest, through which members make their contributions. At the system's apex is the Bombay Panchayat, which uses its funds to reinvest in the community's needs to eliminate poverty, assist in education, and provide medical services.[18]

The Bohra community is known for its rapidly rising influx of prominent professionals, who are inextricably linked to India's ebullient economy. Bohras are also known for their expansive charity in many large-scale renovation projects including the reconstruction of Saifee Hospital in Mumbai, one of the most technologically advanced hospitals in India.

While most Bohras were traditionally traders throughout their dynamic history, today Bohras have emerged as consultants, analysts, and doctors and lawyers. This has been possible primarily due to the synergy and encouragement received from religious and secular education. One of the fundamental requirements for each Bohra is the Misaq at the age of fifteen, a secret oath of allegiance to the head of the community, covering not only religious matters but also encompassing personal, professional, and obligatory aspects of life. This oath cannot be questioned and any transgression from it presumably leads to drastic ramifications. One of the obligatory aspects of the Misaq is a financial donation to the Sydena, or the Chief of the Bohras. The Sydena collects these taxes and has unilateral authority on the application of these funds. However, there is a universal connotation that these funds go to the continued preservation of quality of life for all Bohras, from an educational, health, and career standpoint.

The Sikh community is synonymous with significant achievement in the armed forces and agricultural businesses. While Sikhs constitute only 1.87% of the Indian population, they represent nearly 15% of all ranks in the Indian Army and 20% of its officers. The Sikh Regiment of the Indian Army is regarded as arguably the most accomplished and decorated military unit in the country with 73 Battle Honours, 14 Victoria Crosses, 21 First Class Indian Orders of Merit, and nearly 1600 gallantry awards.

From the standpoint of agriculture, 76% of the approximately 27 million Sikhs live in Punjab, which was home to India's Green Revolution of the 1960s in which the nation went from 'famine to plenty, from humiliation to dignity'. Today, Punjab, primarily due to the predominance of Sikh contribution, is regarded as 'the breadbasket of India' and is statistically the wealthiest state per capita in India, with its citizens earning an annual income three times the national average. The success of Sikhs has been paramount to the advancement of several disciplines and the ubiquity of many institutions, as illustrated by notable Sikh personalities such as the ex-Prime Minister of India

Manmohan Singh, the highest-ranking general in the history of the Indian Air Force, Arjan Singh, and 'the father of fibre optics technology' Dr Narinder Singh Kapany.

A distinctive feature of Sikhism is the advent of mechanisms that allowed the community to holistically and democratically react to changing circumstances affecting their environment. The sixth guru, Guru Hargobind, created the concept of Akal Takht, translated as the 'throne of the timeless one,' which served as the supreme decision-making court for Sikhism. The Sarbat Khalsa, a representative assembly of Sikhs, gathers at the Akal Takht on special festivals when there is a need to discuss and mandate matters affecting the Sikh nation. A gurmata, translated as 'guru's intentions,' is the recognized legislation passed by the Sarbat Khalsa in the presence and with the blessing of Guru Granth Sahib (the final and perpetual Guru of the Sikhs). This gurmata is building upon all Sikhs and may only be passed on a subject affecting the fundamental principles of Sikh religion, including work balance, worship, charitable donations, and community service.

I fondly recall my most intriguing personal experience with a Sikh individual. I was sitting in the car with my secretary when suddenly a young sardar frantically rushed across the road and knocked on our window with a hyper panic. He pleaded, "Sir, *bahut museebat hai*. Please give me INR 2000, and as soon as I reach Punjab, I will return you the money." Seeing the genuine trauma consuming his eyes, and against my secretary's wishes, I gave the young man the money. He made it a point to take down my office address; a gesture my secretary felt was purely symbolic and theatrical.

As we left that intersection, my secretary was relentlessly bombarding me with the opinion that I was duped due to my soft-heartedness. I never had any expectation of being reimbursed; I simply wanted to do the right thing at the dictate of my conscience. Several days later, I was sitting in my office in the midst of several duties, when the peon knocked on my door and handed me a document: it was a money order of INR 2000 from that young man.

I remember simply stopping for a moment, filled with reflections of surprise and warmth as I mentally played back that scene with him. The young man had the integrity, honesty, and commitment to follow-up on his word. From that day forward, that young man has served as my emblematic macrocosm of the Sikh nation. Furthermore, in all my years in India, I've never seen a Sikh beggar on the road, a tell-tale evidence to what altruism, commitment, and human endeavour can produce.

The Khojas regard the sacred person of 'Aga Khan' to be the head of their community and regimentally pay him the dues at births, marriages, burials, and the new moon, through highly efficient dues collecting mechanisms.

Aga Khan has had an illustrious history of innovation and foresight in the community's progress and prominence. According to a historical recount of Aga Khan's consistent impact spanning different eras, 'Systematic use of money, especially by way of offerings to the Imam, is very close to godliness. His Highness saw to it that the money given to him and donated by him for the use of the community was looked after by properly constituted communities of honest men and women. He saw to it that the money was properly put to work and invested. A building society and banking businesses were set up to enable people to own their own houses and businesses. His Highness gave advice and help not only to the great companies he set up, but also to individuals . . . His Highness cared greatly for the health of his people and saw to it that excellent medical and hospital facilities be put in operation with optimum results.'

It dawned upon me that the similarities of these communities and their overwhelming prosperity was not mutually exclusive. Though the Khojas and Bohras are Muslims but the organizational strength and the unity practised by them is not practised by the other Muslim masses at large. More specifically, each of these ethnic communities created all-consuming respect, adherence, and indebtedness to their community's customized infrastructure. Each of these communities abided, adopted, and executed the mantra that 'If you are for your community, in turn, your community is for you.'

RECLAIMING YESTERDAY FOR TOMORROW

I personally felt an overwhelming warmth surge in my heart when I visited the one-thousand-year-old Sankat Mochan Hanuman temple in Varanasi on March 30th, 1995. I had the privilege of performing a havan affectionately welcomed by the mahants, my heart leapt with joy being surrounded with hundreds of worshippers who joined me later in this Parikrama reciting the shlokas, my thoughts raced back into times with reflections of centuries-old Hindu Muslim existence in India which mesmerized me as if I was hearing the surahs from the Holy Quran. The same evening, I was greeted by a sea of people on the ghats of the Shri Jagannathan Mandir, the Kashi Vishwa Pandit Parishad had conferred a doctorate upon me for my achievements in making the classic *Jai Hanuman*.

I have always enjoyed the site of the intermingling of Hindus and Muslims in the dargah of Amir Khusro. It won't be out of place if I mention my wife Zarine, though a staunch Muslim, is also a devotee of Shirdi Sai Baba. It gives me peace and satisfaction to see humanity mingle like colours in a painting—each distinct and unique but coming together to make for pristine beauty. Even in today's India, I've personally experienced the multitude of pluralistic and secular Hindu men and women taking up the cause and protecting the weaker sections of Muslims without fear. Likewise, many established and well-known Muslims have taken up the cause of weaker sections of the Hindus, the commonality between the two communities is Indianism. This is the glue which will keep India alive and take it to the table as one of the four superpowers—India, China, Russia, America, if India so chooses. India has the genius and the wherewithal to sit at the big table if its own people allow it to. The unity of pluralistic secular India is the only glue, which will make it possible to achieve our place in history, if we miss this opportunity we will be sitting on the ground eating the crumbs being thrown to us, instead of sitting on the table.

The lurking danger of hate and communalism for the sake of power will undoubtedly divide and destroy this country. To steer where we are headed, we need to realize where we have been. It is time for us to look back in time and see our contributions to India that Will Durant, the great American historian, saw and so eloquently and definitively concluded: 'It is true that even across the

Himalayan barrier India has sent to the west, such gifts as grammar and logic, philosophy and fables, hypnotism and chess, and above all numerals and the decimal system.'

Muslims entered India as traders and merchants, and thereafter there were invasions. But subsequently they settled down here and opted for this country as their motherland. Muslims were the last catalysts to make India reach the summit of their destiny as a strong and mighty nation. As recently as the beginning of the 18th century, Mughal India represented 27% of the world's Gross Domestic Product.[19]

After the great Mauryan empire and the later Gupta empire, India was divided into multiple principalities and fiefdoms. While some kings went from regional satraps to larger kingdoms, none matched the territorial expanse or the administrative capability of the Mauryans and the Guptas. They fought and conquered each other, expanding and contracting like the water along the tideline for hundreds of years. It was only with the advent of the Muslims which set the beginning of the Delhi Sultanates in the year 1206, and finally with the establishment of the Delhi Sultanate and then Mughal empire that the modern entity with a land and geographical boundary of 'a modern Hindustan' emerged. This was the land border that British empire usurped from the Mughals and which in today's maps delineate the borders of India, Pakistan, Bangladesh, Myanmar, and Afghanistan.

The period of Muslim rule, which began with the later Ghaznavids under different dynasties (i.e. Qutub's Sayed's,

Khilji's, Tughlaq's, Lodi's, and Mughal's) continued until 1857. The credit of creation of 'Hindustan' belonged to the succession of Muslim rulers, who from Delhi, conquered, cajoled, and convinced the disparate Indian principalities to come under one strong central rule. Therefore, one can safely say that the Muslims played a key role and were the catalyst in the creation of Hindustan as one integrated entity, with Delhi as its centre of power establishing India. Most boundaries of today's India were defined by these Muslim rulers. During this period, the contribution of Muslims to India was multidimensional in size and at the same time colossal in content. They came as warriors, travellers, voyagers, traders, and artisans and settled themselves on the Indian soil.

With the establishment of the Delhi Sultanate, new administrative machinery was devised and the system of a strong centralized government with subordinate provincial courts was introduced. It will not be out of place to mention here that the present-day federal system of government is the continuation of the mechanism that was created and introduced by the Sultans and the Mughals, carried forward by the British embellished with their own policies. The present-day council of Ministers is not much different from the Majlis-e-Shura where important affairs of the nation were discussed and adjudicated upon.

Muslims watered the seeds of secularism in India and allowed it to bloom. They did not rule their non-Muslim subjects with Islamic law and permitted the governance of Hindus according to the Vedic canons. The spirit of harmony and cooperation was never absent in society and in religious and social festivities. Esprit de corps was manifest and this recurrent refrain of fraternity could not escape the insightful observation of poet Ghalib, 'The colours of tulip, rose, and narcissus are different. But they are all redolent of spring.'

It is acknowledged by everyone that both Hindus and Muslims imbibed each other's views, thoughts, and customs, resulting in perfect harmony and toleration in different spheres of life; particularly in Indo Muslim mysticism calling for veneration for the truth. Dara Shikoh's veneration for Hindu Philosophy is exemplary in history. His translation of Bhagwad Gita into Persian and the founding of an observatory at Parimahal in Kashmir, reached the high watermark of his love for Indian astronomy and religion, following the stamp of 'Indianness' left by Amir Khusro in music, literature, poetry, wildlife, and agriculture. Sir John Marshall has very aptly remarked: 'Seldom in the history of mankind has the spectacle been witnessed of civilizations, so vast and so strongly developed, yet so and mingling together. The very contrasts which existed between them, the wide divergences in their culture and their religion make the history of their impact peculiarly instructive.' Undoubtedly this was the strength and greatness of the Mughal empire.

This cultural synthesis is also best expressed in Indo Persian literature. With cross-pollination of the two cultures, the whole corpus of Indo Persian literature is not devoid of Indianness. The Indian element in Persian gave a new tone to Persian Ghazal widely known as Ghazal in Indian style or Sabak-e-Hindi. Love for abstract themes, love for the baroque, and novelty in simile and metaphor are the hallmarks of Indian style Persian poetry, in sharp contrast to pure Iranian poetry. Urfi, Naziri, Talib Amuli, Saib, Bedil, Nasir Ali Sarhindi, and Ghalib are all exponents of this original style.

The massive geographic presence of Islam in India can be explained by the tireless activity of Sufi preachers. Sufism, the mystical form of Islam, left a prevailing impact on religious, cultural, and social life in South Asia. Sufi scholars travelling from all over continental Asia were instrumental in the social, economic, and philosophic development of India. Besides preaching in major cities and centres of intellectual thought, Sufis reached out to poor and marginalized rural communities and preached in local dialects such as Urdu, Sindhi, Punjabi versus Persian, Turkish, and Arabic. Sufism emerged as a 'moral and comprehensive socio-religious force' that even influenced other religious traditions such as Hinduism. Their traditions of devotional practices and modest living attracted all people.

Their teachings of humanity, love for God and the Prophet continue to be surrounded by mystical tales and folk songs today. Sufis were firm in abstaining from religious and communal conflict and strived to be peaceful elements of civil society. Furthermore, it is the attitude of accommodation, adaptation, piety, and charisma that continues to help Sufism remain as a pillar of mystical

Islam in India. One of the most revered Sufi saints was Moinuddin Chishti whose Khwaja Gharibnawaz Dargah at Ajmer draws believers from across the religious spectrum. Some of the other famous Sufi saints were Hazrat Nizamuddin Auliya. Like his predecessors, he stressed love as a means of realizing God. For him his love of God implied a love of humanity. His vision of the world was unique with a highly evolved sense of secularity and kindness. Along with him some of the others were Akhi Siraj Aainae Hind and Alauddin Ali Ahmed.

The administrative system prevailing since the Sultanate period continued without much change until the time of Sher Shah Suri. Sher Shah's indefatigable commitment to the improvement of trade, commerce, communication, land revenue system, justice, and the army is extremely momentous in nation-building. The restoration of the road from Indus to Bengal (the Grand Trunk Road, for example), from Agra to Jodhpur and Chittor and Lahore to Multan facilitated the development of trade. His roads and inns in history are called the arteries of the empire in Indian history. Sher Shah's ingeniously planned long and wide roads are the precursor of the present network of roads.

During the reign of the Mughal king Akbar, according to an estimate, more than 600 scholars of Arabic and Persian acquired and disseminated knowledge on the Indian soil, and developed this genre of Persian literature called Sabk-e-Hindi. Shaikh Ali Hazin, a noted Persian scholar, came to India from Iran and wrote: 'I will never leave Benares as the worship of God is unhindered here and every Brahmin traces his lineage to Lord Ram and Lakshman.'

When Akbar expanded his empire, he updated and revised the then existing Indian revenue system. In 1582 AD, he introduced revenue reforms by way of the annual collection of revenue based on soil survey and measurement. The land was duly classified and assessed for the revenue realization. The present-day revenue infrastructure is not much different from the system refined and elaborated by Akbar. The terms Gaz, Tanab, Jarib are still in vogue. The Mughals also paid attention to industry and crafts to the extent that traders even from Europe and other parts of Asia met their demands by sending their requisition.

Akbar's attention to the encouragement of a secular education system and liberal patronage of scholars for rendering Sanskrit classics into Persian and vice-versa, promoted secularism, liberal thinking, and cultural integration. Muslims adorned India with architecturally sound and colonnaded structures. They built magnificent forts, palaces, gardens, fountains, and places of perennial beauty and everlasting charm.

The Fatehpur Sikri is called poetry in marble and the quintessential magic of the redstone is still undiminished in the red-stoned forts at Agra and Delhi. The Taj Mahal, built after Akbar's time, is one of the greatest wonders of the world and still evokes an ethereal shudder at its sight.

Akbar's nine wise men in their respective domain of excellence are famous for their enduring contribution to Indian music, revenue administration, historiography, and promotion of martial arts, medicine, and literature. These prodigies of art, science and literature are Raja Todarmal, Birbal, Raja Mansingh, Tansen, Hakim Hammam, Mulla Do Piaza, Abul Fazal, Faizi, and Abdur Rahim Khankhana and are described by the historians as the nine jewels of Akbar's diadem. The systems of land revenue, soil classification, and musical notations have left an indelible impact on the Indian scene and psyche.

It was the Muslims, who for the first time, introduced mortar of a very enduring kind and superior strength. Dome and arch slab and beam, the use of red and white sandstone and marble in panels, decoration of the walls with floral designs, delicate marble screens, inlay work, and glazed blue tiles were introduced by the Muslims in Indian architecture. The most magnificent buildings constructed by the Muslims are the Qutub Minar, originally of 71.4-metre height, mausoleum of Sher Shah at Saisaram (Bihar), the fort at Agra built in red sandstone, the Panch Mahal at Sikri, Red Fort of Delhi, and Taj at Agra built by Shah Jahan. The chief glory of the Taj is the massive dome and the four slender minarets linking the platform to the main building. These buildings are the pride of the nation and will continue to attract tourists, scholars, and artists from all over the globe. A duty is cast upon the present and coming generation of people to ensure that the pristine beauty of these artefacts is not polluted.

In the 19th century, Sir Syed Ahmad Khan's, a Muslim leader founder of Aligarh Muslim University, stand against dogma, orthodoxy, and intensified effort for scientific temperament quickened the process of modernization of the nation. From amongst his several missionary works, his study of the causes of Indian revolt in 'Asbab-e-Baghawat-e-Hind' was his yeomen service to the nation.

It was a campaign to exonerate the Indians from the blame. Sir Syed had the courage to say that the revolt of 1857 was the result of the British East India Company's aggressive policy of expansion and ignorance of Indian culture. Maulana Altaf Hussain Hali wrote in the biography of Sir Syed: 'As soon as Sir Syed reached Moradabad, he began to write the pamphlet entitled 'The Causes of the Indian Revolt (Asbab-e-Baghawat-e-Hind),' in which he did his best to clear the people of India and especially the Muslims of the charge of Mutiny. In spite of the obvious danger, he made a courageous and thorough report of the accusations people were making against the government and rejected the theory, which the British had invented, to explain the causes of the Mutiny.'

To be precise, the contribution of Muslims in nation-building has been most significant, but after 1947, the glorious past came under a nebulous eclipse and gradually the Muslims sank into social stagnation as well as educational and economic marginalization.

Once the cynosure of the whole world, they are now hurled into a predicament, which needs to be addressed by all those who are sensitive to the fortuitous circumstances responsible for the tragic plight in which the Muslims are labouring and eking out their fleeting existence.

Since 1947, the nation has been indifferent to Muslims'

social and economic backwardness and has ignored the fact that the percentage of Muslim's employment in public and private sector has not been in proportion to their population. During the last few decades, the situation has worsened, particularly of the labourers, artisans, peasants, traders, and the middle-class citizens.

Muslims are now facing an undreamt criticality of their survival; their socio-economic condition presents a spectacle of total gloom and despondency and they are deprived of their due representation in the public and private sector employment. The presence of Muslims in the Indian Administrative Service is only 3%, in the Indian Foreign Service 1.8%, and in the Indian Police Service 4%. A reasonable representation of all communities in the government sector employment is necessary to enhance participatory governance in a pluralistic society and also to inspire confidence in the people in times of commotion and breakdown of law and order. Secure employment in the government not only provides social prestige and security but also influences decision-making process in several ways.

Unfortunately, the employment of Muslims in the Central Public Sector Undertakings at all levels is abysmally low. They are only 2.3% in higher managerial and 2.8% in middle managerial positions. In other positions, they constitute only 3.9%. Furthermore, the representation of Muslims in all the State Government departments and undertakings also does not match with their population share. The State Public Service Commission's hold their respective recruitments and the share of Muslims in all these selections does not exceed 2.1%, according to the figures collected by the Sachar Committee.

In the National Security Agencies, including the three wings of the defence forces, the position of Muslim participation is extremely disheartening. Out of 1.9 million employees, the share of Muslims is as low as 3.6% at the A and B levels and 4.6% at C and D levels. From an academia perspective, according to the data received by the Sachar Committee from 129 universities and 84 colleges consisting of a total of 137,000 employees, Muslims are just 3.7% in the teaching faculty and 5.4% in the non-teaching sector. Now the number of universities and colleges has increased manifold, but the marginal presence of Muslims in the regular employment in these institutions has remained unchanged.

According to the 2001 Sachar Commission Report on the Muslim reality in India, the literacy rate among Muslims was only 59%, far below the national average of 65%. In addition, as many as 25% of Muslim children ages 6-14 have either never attended a school or have dropped out. Furthermore, a comparison across all religious demographics reveals consistently lower levels of mean years of schooling and higher dropout rates for the Muslim community.

What is even more problematic about this phenomenon is the steady increase in the dropout rate of this trend. The disparity in graduation attainment rates is widening since the 1970s between Muslims and all other religious groups, to the point where today, in terms of premier colleges in India, only 1 out of 25 undergraduate students and only 1 out of 50 graduate students is a Muslim.[20]

Furthermore, and most alarmingly, Muslims categorized as literate were not presented with enough opportunities to apply their reading and writing skills to real-world scenarios in their post-education experiences, and as a result, a substantial portion reverted to illiteracy within 4-5 years of leaving the school. How can there be an opportunity for this critical mass of fellow Muslims without education? The answer, of course, is that it's impossible, and this is evident in the lack of employment prospects, benefits, and careers for the Muslims.

A significantly larger proportion of Muslim workers are engaged in self-employment activities and, as discussed above, their participation in formal sector employment (both private and public) is significantly less than the national average, even compared to the traditionally disadvantaged communities. On average, compared to all other religious groups, Muslim workers receive lower salaries in both public and private sector jobs. Employment studies from several reputable sources clearly show on average, Muslim workers to be the most susceptible to not receiving social security and health benefits as well as being most vulnerable to being hired without written contractual agreements.

Clearly, these are devastating facts with very detrimental ramifications and far-reaching consequences. Muslim India, by virtue of its size, has been afforded a powerful platform to inspire Muslims all over the world. Yet, as a whole, why are we going in the wrong direction? Muslims have demonstrated profound greatness across all notable disciplines and furthermore, India has numerous enlightened and educated Muslims, who have undoubtedly left iconic stamps on their respective fields. So why isn't today's Muslim India, in contrast to yesterday's Muslim India with its rich library of profound and transcendent accomplishment, uniformly an essential asset to the nation? In order to unlock that answer, we need to delve into the heart of pragmatic questioning, namely, what are the causes for this lack of education?

There are the more superficially unilateral answers, practical in nature, such as lack of access. It is evidently true that very few schools exist beyond the primary level in Muslim localities. As a result, these localities are heavily reliant on the teachings in madrasas, often the case being that these madrasas are the only educational option available to the children, especially those in poor areas.

Unfortunately, many of these rural madrasas but not all are harbingers of extremist philosophies that exploit destitute and impressionable souls into a vortex of violence, destructive behaviour, and terrorist activity. Thus, streamlining madrasas with a multidisciplinary curriculum (i.e. Natural and Social Sciences, Mathematics, English, and Hindi in addition to religious studies) and modernized educational tools such as computers 'will expectedly help produce more enlightened, socially aware, and vocationally equipped students through the madrasa system'. This initiative will have a parallel duality of success, namely, reducing the poisonous influences of criminal behaviour while enhancing professional competitiveness and outlook.

While this is certainly a valid narrative, it grossly overlooks the heart of the problem. There is a much deeper sentiment at play, one that is a simmering inferno at the undercurrent of Muslim India's psyche: Muslims feel piercingly alienated in today's post-Partition India, and have carried that feeling since the fatal stages of the nation's independence.

According to the Sachar Commission Report, 'the perception of being discriminated against is overpowering amongst a wide cross-section of Muslims resulting in collective alienation'. What is most profound is that the depth of this alienation spans across cultural, social, and educational boundaries. The heart of this alienation lies in a very raw human emotion, one of insecurity, which rears its overpowering head when an established sense of identity hasn't been achieved. This lack of distinct identity could not be truer for Muslim India. The Muslims are juggling the double-edged sword of being labelled as 'anti-national' and simultaneously as having to be 'appeased'.

The backlash of destructive behaviour caused by certain rural madrasas leads to the universal branding of Muslims being 'anti-national'. Furthermore, this powerful force of human misconception is being compounded with the external resentment towards having to 'appease' Muslims by having to adopt affirmative-action policies for them, despite their 'anti-national' behaviour and their relative lack of education. As a result of these sentiments, it's only natural for Muslims to develop cultural inferiority complexes.[21]

As the Sachar Commission Report stated, 'Muslims live with an inferiority complex as every bearded man is considered an ISI agent.' It brings me grave sadness every time I am made aware of incidents when innocent Muslims are categorized as villains, terrorists, or criminals due to their outward appearance or presentation.

Due to these cultural insecurities, this alienation manifests itself into the notion of 'ghettoization'. Namely, from a social perspective, Muslims out of fear for their safety and peace of mind, would rather live in ghettos, essentially trading off the comfort and advantages of infrastructural benefits such as sanitation, electricity, education, transportation, and banking facilities, for the safety in living with large numbers of fellow Muslims. More notably, for a critical mass of Muslim women, the jurisdiction of the term 'safety' is explicitly defined as the boundaries between one's home and one's community.

Adding to the uneasiness of this type of existence is that historically, ghettos are not very stable places to live from the standpoint of social unrest and educational outlook.

As history tends to be a periodic function of time, numerous social boycotts and demonstrations by Muslims over the course of the nation's history, have forced Muslims to repeatedly migrate, thereby further feeding this notion of insecurity and a lack of permanence. Additionally, this volatility of frequent movement gives legitimacy and prominence to the types of misguided madrasas as mentioned previously, thereby creating this infinite loop of fostering internal reflections of alienation and external perceptions of 'antinationalism' and 'appeasement'.

What is even more troubling is that this alienation has even entered the educational domain. The plethora of a school's religious content, from textbooks to course portions, to its ideological ethos itself, has become a growing concern for Muslims, as it uniquely disadvantages students not from those particular backgrounds and makes these students feel isolated. Furthermore, the resistance by state governments to recognize minority educational institutions as a viable degree-granting entities continues to concern Muslims as it once again demonstrates alienation and a lack of equality.

Solving this intricately complicated problem involves effort from both the nation as well as from Muslim citizens. From the standpoint of the government, it is essential to develop and cultivate trust, respect, and collaboration with the Muslim citizens of India, so moving forward we can overcome the current fear, scepticism, and negativity Muslims have of governmental institutions, such as the police.

As the Sachar Committee stated, a near-unanimous Muslim sentiment is that 'whenever any incident occurs, Muslim boys are picked up by the police.' From a tangible implementation standpoint, it is the duty, responsibility, and civic obligation of state governments to provide affordable, high-quality education via the mechanized formal educational system to help reverse the unfortunate reality of Muslims having the highest unemployment rates and lowest graduation rates of any other religious group

Article 28-32 of the Indian Constitution states that: 'Any ethnic group can create educational institutions to preserve cultural identity; State cannot discriminate these institutions in terms of allocation of funds'. However, tragically today Muslim educational centres are not being registered nor recognized as such.[22]

Keeping politics aside, Prime Minister Modi is in serious pursuit of making India great again. This can only happen if there is peace and tranquillity and an educated class of people standing behind to support him in his endeavours of nation-building. We have in the past trusted many political parties and we must now give BJP an opportunity to prove and fulfil its promises. It's time now to take the initiative of the recent policy of the Government of India, announced by Mukhtar Abbas Naqvi, the Union Minister of Minority Affairs, to train two hundred teachers to teach in the madrasas. It is believed that the government is in dialogue with Jamia Milia and Delhi University and few other institutions for the targeted first phase. The 'Bridge Course' will be available from eighth standard onwards so that the children passing out from madrasas can at least get formal secondary, or higher secondary school degrees. I welcome the idea of introducing formal education in other subjects like English, Hindi, science, maths, computer science, etc., as this was in existence throughout the history of the madrasas worldwide. The initiative taken by the Modi government to re-introduce all subjects in the madrasa is a commendable move. I am confident they will escalate and reinforce this move with greater number of teachers and include more educational institutions to cater to this huge Indian-Muslim population.[23]

I fervently appeal to all Muslim organizations in India to seriously engage with the government and lend their support in furthering this initiative towards education. The onus lies on the Indian-Muslim youth to whole-heartedly co-operate with the government's initiative in their own interest as a good education is the only way forward to reclaim your yesterday for tomorrow . . .

Sanjay Khan in *The Sword Of Tipu* Sultan in Mysore

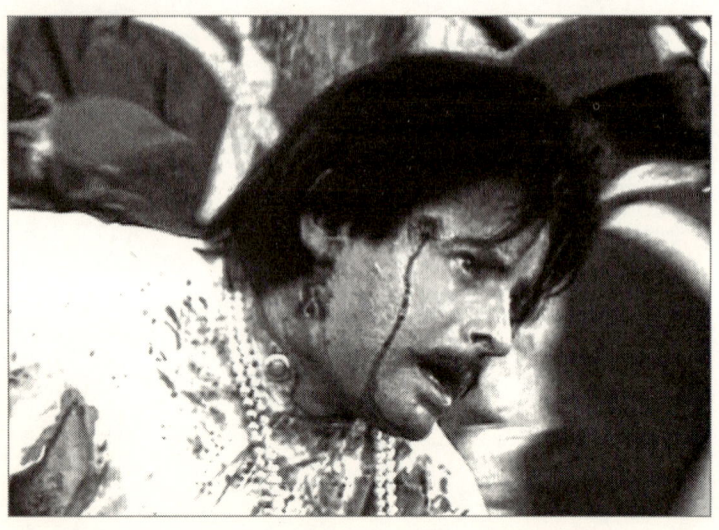

Sanjay Khan in the climax of *The Sword Of Tipu Sultan*

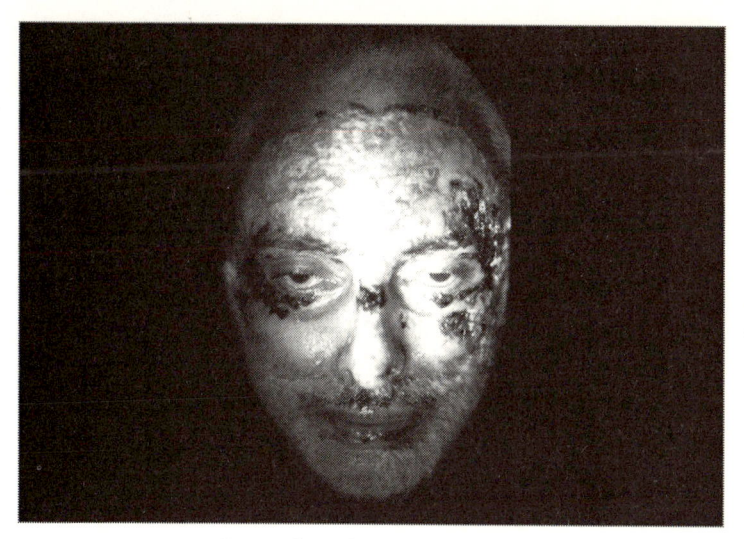

Sanjay Khan after the fire tragedy

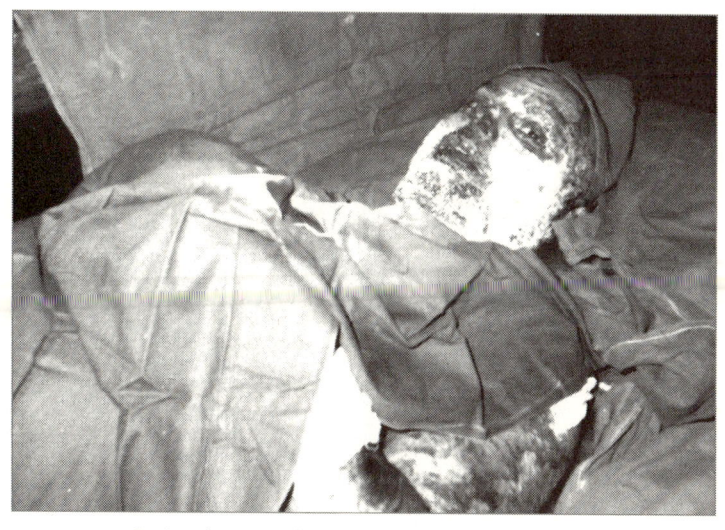

Sanjay Khan at Jaslok Hospital after the fire tragedy

Sanjay Khan, Bhushan Jeevan, Utkarsha Naik on the sets of *The Great Maratha*

Sanjay Khan on the sets of *Jai Hanuman*

Sanjay Khan directing *The Great Maratha*

Sanjay Khan, Irfan Khan, Raju Shrestha on the sets of *Jai Hanuman*

Sanjay Khan reading Koran

॥ श्रीः ॥

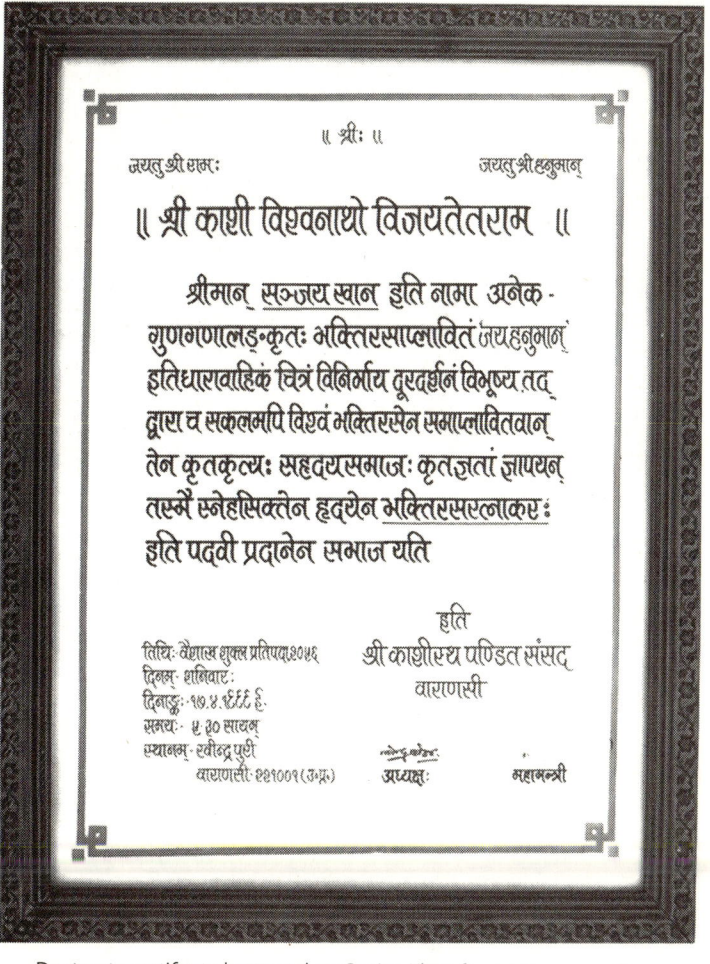

जयतु श्री रामः   जयतु श्री हनुमान्

॥ श्री काशी विश्वनाथो विजयतेतराम् ॥

श्रीमान् सञ्जय खान इति नामा अनेक-
गुणगणालङ्कृतः भक्तिरसप्लावितं जयहनुमान्
इतिधारावाहिकं चित्रं विनिर्माय दूरदर्शनं विभूष्य तद्-
द्वारा च सकलमपि विश्वं भक्तिरसेन समाप्लावितवान्
तेन कृतकृत्यः सहृदयसमाजः कृतज्ञतां ज्ञापयन्
तस्मै स्नेहसिक्तेन हृदयेन भक्तिरसरत्नाकरः
इति पदवी प्रदानेन सभाजयति

इति
श्री काशीस्थ पण्डित संसद्
वाराणसी

तिथिः वैशाख शुक्ल प्रतिपदा २०५६
दिनम्ः शनिवारः
दिनाङ्कः १७.४.१९९९ ई.
समयः ५.३० सायम्
स्थानम्ः रवीन्द्रपुरी
वाराणसी २२१००१ (उ.प्र.)

अध्यक्षः   महामन्त्री

Doctorate certificate bestowed on Sanjay Khan for *Jai Hanuman* from
Shri Kashi Vishwanath Mandir Trust

Sanjay Khan receiving National Citizen's Award from Mother Teresa

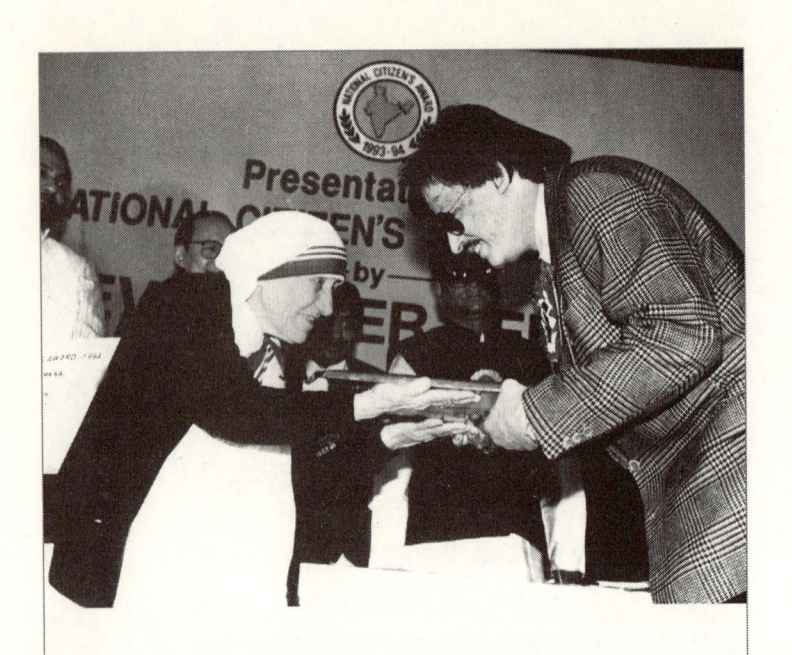

Sanjay Khan, Micheal Jackson, and Zarine Khan

His Higness King of Morocco and Sanjay Khan

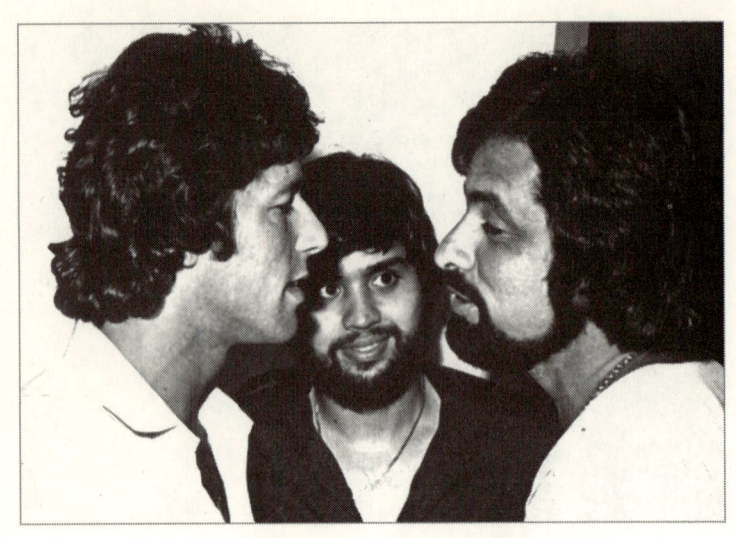

Sanjay Khan with Pakistan cricket captain Imran Khan

President Yasser Arafat, then president of the
Palestinian National Authority, with Sanjay Khan

Zayed Khan and Sanjay Khan with HH King Birendra of Nepal

Sanjay Khan with Prime Minister of Mauritius
Sir Seoosagar Ramghulam

Sanjay Khan and Prime Minister Atal Bihari
Vajpayee on the sets of *The Great Maratha*

Prime Minister Narendra Modi with Sanjay Khan and Zarine Khan

Uttar Pradesh Chief Minister Akhilesh Yadav with Sanjay Khan

Sanjay Khan and Gulam Nabi Azad

Prime Miniter Indira Gandhi with Sanjay Khan

Sanjay Khan with Prime Minister of India, Shri Rajiv Gandhi and
Yuri Vorenstov, Soviet Ambassador to India, 1982

Sanjay Khan, Bob Cristo, and students of a school in Rajasthan

Sanjay Khan inspecting the construction site of
Golden Palms Hotel in Bangalore

Sanjay Khan, Zarine Khan, and Dr Asad Madni

Sanjay Khan with brother Feroz Khan

Sanjay Khan with Jagat Guru Swarupaandji

Sanjay Khan with the pandits of Hare Rama Hare Krishna

SECTION IV

SECTION IV

DISTINGUISHED MUSLIM WOMEN

The status of women in Indian society is a much-debated subject and various points of view have been put forth defending or condemning the position occupied by or imposed upon them. The position of women under Islam has been the subject of repeated controversies among educated Muslims ever since they came under the impact of Western liberalization, ranging from the rigid interpretation of the sharia under the Taliban to equally radical implementation of banning of religious symbology in public—like those implemented by France in banning the headscarf. Both these extremes encompass a middle ground where the role of women in Muslim society is debated and defined. However, a careful study of Islamic rules and laws shows that behind the veil of distorted facts, the rights of Muslim women are in accordance with the rules of equality.

We are facing bewildering times. At one end of the spectrum, women are commanding the pinnacle of technologies—the space shuttle in the most challenging of conditions, the outer space—while at another end of the spectrum women are barbarically stoned to death for perceived infringement of Islam's guidance. It shocks and shames me to realize that my Muslim sisters are one of the most oppressed group in the world, be it the zealotry of the Taliban or its medusa like avatar, the so-called ISIS to the radical diktats.

In India, where thankfully radicalism has yet to spread its tentacles deep into the society, worrying examples of institutionalized violence towards women are visible. One only has to flip through the paper to read the articles about the Khap panchayats punishing women along caste lines, or the diktats of the Ulema banning cell phones and trousers. As a father of three daughters, it pains and revolts me to see the degree of denigration that the women in our society face today.

This discrimination is unjustified. It has been proven again and again that women are as capable in every field as men. Be they astronauts like the late Kalpana Chawla or Indra Nooyi, ex-CEO of Pepsi, or Kiran Mazumdar Shaw of Indian pharmaceutical giant Biocon. In the field of sports, Indian women are consistently outperforming men in the international arena with stars like Deepika Pallikal, Saina Nehwal, Mary Kom, Sania Mirza, PV Sindhu, Nuzhat Parveen, Mitali Raj, Harman Preet Kaur, and Harleen Deol of the women cricket team of India.

One inspiring example that has blossomed into this world is the story of Malala Yousafzai from Pakistan who fought for her right to get an education. Her courage and fortitude almost resulted in her death when at the age of fifteen the heinous Pakistan Taliban tried to assassinate her. Grievously wounded, she was treated in Birmingham and made a miraculous recovery.

Malala's crime was that she wanted the right to education for herself and others. Her passionate belief that every individual has a right to their own destiny and the key to that lies in education brought her face to face with some of the most cruel and barbaric forces of fundamentalism. She fought and survived these forces and continues to lead the charge for women's education. She continues to inspire the youth of the world to take the right path—the path of truth, courage, and conviction.

Muslim women are discriminated against on two fronts—firstly for being a woman in our highly hierarchical and chauvinistic patriarchal society and secondly for being part of the 'religious minority'. The result is that a large section of women are denied access to fundamental rights and in the process face various forms of oppression, either knowingly or unknowingly. India's progressive Constitution and several 'pro-women' laws and judgments have failed to achieve justice for women from minorities primarily because they lack the knowledge of their rights and the effective support in accessing those rights. The legal system and the law enforcement is still not supportive of women, especially women from the 'minority' communities.

To protect the disparate and diverse rights of our various 'minority' communities, our far-sighted Constitution laid down, through Articles 25 to 30, the rights to religious practices and belief, culture and language for all communities, and has, therefore, made India a truly democratic and pluralist nation. But a gap exists between thought and action, law and implementation, intentions and actual realization. The communities continue to face several problems and ironically specific Minority rights have, at least indirectly, created barriers for gender equality.

In India, each community is, in matters relating to family, inheritance, adoption, etc., governed by the Personal Laws of the community. Although protection of the Personal Law was not considered as the fundamental right of the community or its members, yet, the right to culture, granted to communities, has been used to advocate non-interference of the state in the Personal Laws of communities. A careful study of the individual community's Personal Laws reveal that they are generally biased against women, and non-interference in matters of Personal Law has obstructed the process of ensuring gender equality for all sections of the population.

Hasan and Menon (2005) studied about the education of Muslim girls by doing a logical 'Comparison of Five Indian Cities' and found some similarities and many disparities regarding the issue. The issue of educational disparities was among the most striking factors. Among Muslims, Shariff (1995) said, the literacy rate is about 59%, compared with the over 65% among Indians as a whole.

On average, a Muslim child attends school for three years and four months, against a national average of four years. Less than 4% of Muslims graduate from school, compared with 6% of the total population. Less than 2% of the students at the elite Indian Institutes of Technology are Muslim. Equally revealing, only 4% of Muslim children attend madrasas, Shariff pointed out.[24]

The Socio-Economic Plight of the Indian-Muslims[25]

Indian-Muslims face mainly three basic problems, which can be divided into many subgroups.

These problems more or less cause hurdles in the process of aspirations and targets: educational, economic, and socio-political.

The first and foremost problem is the absence of a vision, which cannot be conceived without genuine leadership. The present Muslim leadership seems to be fragile or they are the spokespersons of the ideology of some political or a few socio-economic groups.

The second problem of Indian-Muslims is lack of security. Riots and communal violence have become a sad reality of India's life and the majority of the victims of riots in India are Muslims.

The next problem of the Muslim community is income. Although the economic and social situation of Muslims is not the same throughout India, one cannot deny the fact that poverty adversely affects the actual educational development of the community. In 1999, a team of researchers at the National Council of Applied Economic Research (NCAER), led by Shariff (2010) published the results of a nationwide survey of 33,000 households. This study collated information according to socio-economic status, caste, and religion. Which clearly shows that a larger proportion of Muslims than other religious minorities suffer from low levels of consumption.

Muslims generally are disadvantaged and the issue has already been connected with various socio-economic factors: poverty (Bhagat and Praharaj 2005, Unni 2001), land ownership (Kulkarni 2002), and income (Khandker, 1992). Muslims suffer from poverty more than other communities in India such as Hindus, Christians, and Sikhs. About 23% of India's total population is poor compared to 31% of Muslims.

In urban areas, Muslims experience the highest poverty rate (38.4%) compared to scheduled castes and tribes (36.4%), other backward castes (25.1%), upper-caste Hindus (8.3%), and other minorities (12.2%). Muslims in rural areas are slightly better off, experiencing the second-highest poverty rate (26.9%). Scheduled castes and tribes have the highest poverty rate (34.8%), while other backward castes (19.5%), upper-caste majority group, Hindus (9.0%) and other minorities (14.3%), experience considerably lower poverty rates (Government of India, 2006). Jaffrey (2005) especially studies the problems of girl's education in Uttar Pradesh (the largest state/province in India) and revealed many factors that were quite similar to the Indian scenario.

In rural areas, land ownership is an important basis for material well-being. There are more landless Muslims compared to Hindus. Among rural dwellers, 35% of Muslims are landless compared to 28% of Hindus (Shariff, 1995).

Muslims also experience disadvantage in employment compared to Hindus. The work participation rate, defined as the percentage of workers to the total population, is 31.3% for Muslims compared to 40.4% for Hindus. In addition, Muslims are underrepresented in both the public and private sectors (Hasan, 2005) and are largely confined to non-farm self-employment (Das, 2002).

Problems of Muslim Women Entrepreneurs in India[26]

The basic problem of a woman entrepreneur is that she is a woman. Women entrepreneurs face the following set of problems specific to women entrepreneurs. These are summarized as follows:

1. Shortage of Finance: Women and small entrepreneurs always suffer from inadequate fixed and working capital. Owing to lack of confidence in women's ability, male members in the family do not like to risk their capital in ventures run by women. Banks have

also taken negative attitude while lending to women entrepreneurs. Thus, women entrepreneurs rely often on personal saving and loans from family and friends.

2. Shortage of Raw Material: Women entrepreneurs find it difficult to procure material and other necessary inputs. The prices of many raw materials are quite high.

3. Inadequate Marketing Facilities: Most of the women entrepreneurs depend on intermediaries for marketing their products. It is very difficult for women entrepreneurs to explore the market and to make their product popular. For women, the market is a 'chakravyuh'.

4. Keen Competition: Women entrepreneurs face tough competition from male entrepreneurs and also from organized industries. They cannot afford to spend large sums on advertisement.

5. High Cost of Production: High prices of material, low productivity, underutilization of capacity, etc., accounts for the high cost of production. The government assistance and subsidies would not be sufficient for survival.

6. Family Responsibilities: Management of family may be more complicated than the management of the business. Hence, she cannot put her full involvement in the business. Occupational backgrounds of the family and education level of the husband have a direct impact on the development of women entrepreneurship.

7. Low Mobility: One of the biggest handicaps for the women entrepreneur is her inability to travel from one place to another for business purposes. A single woman asking for a room is looked upon with suspicion. Sometimes licensing authorities, labour officials, and sales tax officials may harass them.
8. Lack of Education: About 60% of women are still illiterate in India. There exists a belief that investing in woman's education is a liability, not an asset. Lack of knowledge and experience creates further problems in the setting up and operation of the business.
9. Low Capacity to Bear Risks: Women lead a protected life dominated by the family members. She is not economically independent. She may not have the confidence to bear the risk alone. If she cannot bear risks, she can never be an entrepreneur.
10. Social Attitudes: Women do not get equal treatment in a male-dominated society. Wherever she goes, she faces discrimination. The male ego stands in the way of success of women entrepreneurs. Thus, the rigid social attitudes prevent a woman from becoming a successful entrepreneur.
11. Low Need for Achievement: Generally, a woman will not have a strong need for achievement. Every woman suffers from the painful feeling that she is forced to depend on others in her life. Her preconceived notions about her role in life inhibit achievement and independence.

12. Lack of Training: A women entrepreneur from middle class starts her first entrepreneurial venture in her late thirties or early forties due to her commitments towards children. Her biggest problem is the lack of sufficient business training.
13. Lack of Information: Women entrepreneurs sometimes are not aware of technological developments and other information on subsidies and concessions available to them. They may not know how to get loans, industrial estates, raw materials, etc.

Compared to United States of America (25.5%), Ghana (46.4%) United Kingdom (25%), Indonesia (25.2%) and Brazil (27.2%), the percentage of Indian women entrepreneurs is the lowest at 11%.[27]

The Koran propounds equality of man and woman and admonishes those who oppress and ill-treat women. It goes on to say:

'And for women are rights over men similar to those of men over women.' (Noble Koran 2:228)

Prior to the Koranic teachings, the situation of the pagan Arab women was those of a third-class citizen. There are recorded reports of female foeticide by burying the excess female children alive and the treatment of women as mere chattels and objects of sexual pleasure possessing no rights and position whatsoever.

The teachings of the Koran were therefore revolutionary. The Koran goes on to say: 'Women are the twin halves of men' and celebrates the essential unity of men and women in a most beautiful simile: *They (your wives) are your garment and you are the garment for them.'* (Noble Koran 2:187).

The Prophet wanted to put a stop to the cruelties meted out to women. He preached kindness towards them and told his followers: *'Fear Allah in respect of women.'* And, *'The best of you are they who behave best to their wives.'* And, *'A Muslim must not hate his wife, and if he be displeased with one bad quality in her, let him be pleased with one that is good.'* And, *'The more civil and kinder a Muslim is to his wife, the more perfect in faith he is.'*

In the eyes of Islam, a woman has a completely independent personality. She can make any contract or bequest in her own name, is entitled to inherit her positions as a mother, as a wife, as a sister, and as a daughter. She has perfect liberty to choose her husband.

The Prophet states emphatically that the rights of the mother are paramount. A man asked the Prophet once: *'O Messenger of Allah, who is the person who has the greatest rights on me with regards to kindness and attention?'*

He replied, 'Your mother.'
'Then who?'
He replied, 'Your mother.'
'Then who?'
He replied the third time, 'Your mother.'
'Then who?'
He replied, 'Your father.'

'O mankind! Reverence your Guardian-Lord who created you from a single person, created, of like nature, his mate, and from this

pair scattered (like seeds) countless men and women. Reverence Allah, through whom you demand your mutual (rights), and reverence the wombs (that bore you); for Allah ever watches over you.' (Noble Koran 4:1)

Equality of men and women and non-discrimination on the basis of gender constitutes one of the vital human rights concerns, finding expression in all international instruments as well as in the Indian Constitution. In reality, however, Muslim women in India constitute one of the most deprived groups who are unable to fully enjoy their equal rights. Their deprivation and vulnerability derive from the following sources, namely cultural and religious, legal, socio-economic and educational, and violence against Muslim women.

The problems of Muslim women are many-sided and closely related to the problems of the Muslim society as a whole. Therefore, to improve the condition of Muslim women, one will have to solve the problems of the Muslim society at large. A step in the right direction would be for the Muslims today not be limited by the constraints of limited interpretation, but reinterpret the teachings of Islam in accordance with the needs and circumstances of our own age and needs. All interpretation should aim for the betterment of human consciousness, human rights, and human dignity.

The laws regarding women, drawn up during the medieval period by the jurists, though based on interpretations of the scriptures, are unlikely to be accepted by women today. They silently or openly challenge their subordinate position. They rightfully demand equal status with men. A careful study of history has shown that despite attempts to keep women in subservient roles, many have risen and garnered positions of reverence.

For example, Nusaybah bint Ka'b Al-Ansariyah, who was born in today's Saudi Arabia and died circa 634, was the first women warrior of Islam. In the battle of Udth, every time danger approached the Prophet she hastened to protect him. Muhammad (pbuh) noticed this, and later said, *'Wherever I turned, to the left or the right, I saw her fighting for me.'*

There are many other notable Muslim women whose actions have rippled across the timelines of history. For example, Fatima al-Fihri born in Morocco in the late 9th century was the founder of the oldest degree-granting university in the world. After inheriting a large fortune, she donated her money to pious work that would benefit the community. With her wealth, she built the Al Qarawiyyin mosque. From the 10th to 12th century, the mosque developed into a university: Al Qarawiyyin University. Today, the Guinness Book of World Records and UNESCO recognize this university to be the oldest continuously operating institution of higher education in the world.

In more recent times, we have Nana Asma'u of Nigeria (1793-1864), who was born as a princess but devoted her time as a poet and teacher. She was fluent in Arabic, Fulfulde, Hausa, and Tamacheq and well-versed in Arabic, Greek, and Latin classics. In 1830, she formed a group of female teachers who journeyed throughout the region to educate women in poor and rural regions. With the republication of her works which underscore women's education, she has become a rallying point for African women. In 19th century West Africa, Nana Asma'u was a leading Islamic scholar, poet, teacher, and an exceptionally prolific Muslim female writer who wrote more than sixty works. Today, in northern Nigeria, Islamic women's organizations, schools, and meeting halls are frequently named in her honour. This is particularly ironic as the scourge of ultra-fundamentalist Islamic group—Boko Haram, a latest internationally inspired terrorist organization—is sweeping across Nigeria and specifically targets women and their right towards education.

In India, the lores of Chand Bibi and Razia Sultana along with others continue to impress and inspire us today. Chand Bibi or Chand Sultana (1550-1599) was the regent of Bijapur and put up a strong resistance to Emperor Akbar in defending Ahmednagar. Razia Sultana (1205-1240) was the first and last woman ruler of the Delhi Sultanate. Razia Sultana is said to have pointed out that the spirit of religion was more important than its parts, and that even the Islamic Prophet Muhammad spoke against overburdening the non-Muslims. Razia established schools, academies, centres for research, and public libraries that included the works of ancient philosophers along with the Koran and the traditions of Muhammad. Hindu works in the sciences, philosophy, astronomy, and literature were reportedly studied in schools and colleges.

Begum Hazrat Mahal, also called Begum of Awadh, was the second wife of Nawab Wajid Ali Shah. History records that at that time Begum Hazrat Mahal ruled the largest area of rebel land, commanded the most significant rebel force of the 1857 first war of independence, and held out the longest against the British—an overwhelming modern force with long supply lines, difficult for anyone to confront and who would eventually bring to bear formidable imperial forces to crush Lucknow. The Begum rallied and excited all Awadh, her extraordinary courage with her fiery oratory made the chiefs swear alliance to her which prompted the Begum to declare undying war against the British.

Azizan, another freedom fighter, was born in Lucknow in 1832. It is said that she lived with Umrao Jaan in Sarangi Mahal. On June 4, 1857, when Nana Sahib called Hindus and Muslims to unite for the cause of freedom and join him, she left home and joined the freedom movement. She was skilled in the art of war and organized a battalion of women whom she taught how to use arms. She even collected information about the British and passed it on to the freedom fighters. She was caught and brought in front of General Havelock who offered to forgive her if she confessed to all her faults. But Azizan rejected the proposal, spurned his offer of mercy, and stood committed to destroying the British. With scornful disdain General Havelock ordered his soldiers to open fire, and so the bullets pierced through her body.

The ladies of Meerut were so inspired by this

courageous act by Azizan that they sent their bangles to the sepoys in the barracks to remind them of their duty. The soldiers were further aroused and infuriated with the British, which prompted Mangal Pandey to shoot and kill his officer, engulfing the entire country into the first war of independence in 1857.

Abadi Begam, Zubaida Daoodi, Amjadi Begam, Nisat-Ul-Nisa Begam, Razia Khatoon, Sadat Bano Kichlew, Zulekha Begum, and Karuna Asaf Ali Khan are few of the Indian-Muslim women freedom fighters who cannot be forgotten for their audacity in their fight for their freedom of India.

If you go by the just mentioned factual history, you'll agree women have always been at the forefront standing shoulder to shoulder with their husbands. They not only carried out the responsibilities of raising children and keeping home but they also joined their husbands in the call of duty in the service of the nation—some losing their lives and some losing all. It is ironic that women empowerment is a recent phenomenon.

In 2003, Shirin Ebadi (1947-present) became the first Muslim woman to receive the Nobel Peace Prize. As a judge in Iran, she was the first woman to achieve chief justice status. However, she was dismissed from this position after the 1979 Revolution. As a lawyer, Shirin has taken on many controversial cases and as a result, has been arrested numerous times. Her activism has been predicated on her view that: 'An interpretation of Islam that is in harmony with equality and democracy is an authentic expression of faith. It is not religion that binds women, but the selective diktats of those who wish them cloistered.'

Taking Shirin's interpretation to heart, in 2006, Anousheh Ansari, an American-Iranian engineer (1966-present), became the first Muslim woman in space. When asked about what she hoped to achieve on her spaceflight, she said, "I hope to inspire everyone, especially young people, women and young girls all over the world and in Middle Eastern countries that do not provide women with the same opportunities as men—to not give up their dreams and to pursue them. It may seem impossible to them at times. But I believe they can realize their dreams if they keep it in their hearts, nurture it, and look for opportunities and make those opportunities happen."

The rights of women have assumed an enhanced significance in modern times in general, and in the Islamic world in particular. Islam supervises the entire lifespan of a woman in sufficient detail. Islam also contributes to the improvement of the status of women in many ways—for example, meting out good treatment and respecting a foster mother, by making a woman the mistress of her own property with no interference, by giving her the right to claim divorce on certain grounds, permission to hold any public office, remarriage, encouragement to study. While these aspects are sufficiently detailed out in the scriptures, unfortunately, in actual practice, the tendency seems to be to overlook or misinterpret the principles and orders of the Koran and consequently to accord to the woman an inferior status.

Asghar Ali Engineer, in one of the leading Muslim journals, said that the minorities were often stereotyped as 'fanatical' and 'fundamentalists' and the acts of few individuals would be seen as of the entire community. Even if a religious leader issued any appeal to the Muslims, it will be described by a loaded word like fatwa, binding on all Muslims. One example is the way the Shah Bano case was projected in the media, including the secular media; it gave an impression as if only Indian-Muslims mistreat their women and deny them their basic rights. That Islam treats women better than many other religious traditions or legal systems, was never brought out in any analysis—media or otherwise.

The Shah Bano case is a classic example of how an issue that should have been solved under the strict guidelines of the law was turned into a political checker game with the religious denotations becoming the pawns in this case. Shah Bano, a 60-year-old woman went to court asking maintenance from her husband who had divorced her and the court ruled in her favour. Shah Bano was entitled to maintenance from her ex-husband under Section 125 of the Criminal Procedure Code, like any other Indian woman. The judgment was not the first granting divorced Muslim woman maintenance under Section 125 but the orthodox Muslims led by vocal Ulemas deemed this verdict an attack on Islam.

Being an election year, the hyper-sensitive government,

came in under the pressure and hastily enacted the Muslim Women (Protection of Rights on Divorce) Act, 1986. The most controversial provision of the Act was that it gave a Muslim woman the right to maintenance for the period of iddat (about three months) after the divorce, and shifted the onus of maintaining her to her relatives or the Wakf Board (charitable trust or trust law). The sword, as they say, fell on the valiant Arif Mohammed Khan, a close friend of Rajiv Gandhi and a cabinet minister, who with sheer frustration and on principle submitted his resignation in the defence of Shah Bano. Arif Mohammed Khan is a true Indian Muslim patriot and a man of principle. I was truly heartened to read in the newspapers that the Modi government has appointed him governor of Kerala. Over the years I have often wondered why this talented man was not used in public service.

The Act was seen as discriminatory as it denied divorced Muslim women the right to basic maintenance which women of other faiths had recourse to under secular law. This law is not only discriminatory but also institutionalizes the primacy of the patriarchal societal norms.

To summarize, the role of women in Islam has been misunderstood due to the general ignorance of the true Islamic system, the Islamic way of life, and because of the distortions of the media. The need of the hour is to come together to find a new approach which will overcome the shortcomings and limitations. It is now necessary for the Indian-Muslim women to realize and enjoy their full human rights and start a process of reform within the community and empowerment through affirmative action programmed for greater access to education, economic, and political institutions and opportunities.

The 21st century will be the century of democracy and human rights and India can be justly proud of being a democratic nation on the path to provide human rights to all its citizens. The challenge is to further deepen and consolidate this. As the quality of democracy improves, all communities should get all opportunities for their own creative contribution to the process of nation-building. The majority should realize that the more secure the 'minorities' feel, the more they will contribute to nation-building. A new approach, based on 'faith and customary religious laws' that uphold basic human values, will lead to the end of exploitation of Indian-Muslim women.

Even with the lenient definition of 'literate' and 'educated'—being generously defined as being able to read and write a sentence or two—more than 50% of Indian-Muslim women are illiterate. The situation in the northern states and specifically the rural belts are even more dismal, with the numbers touching a high of 85% and above in some places.

Historically, the world over, women played an important role in the foundation of many Islamic educational institutions, such as Fatima al-Fihri's founding of the University of Al Qarawiyyin in 859 CE. This continued through to the Ayyubid dynasty in the 12th and 13th centuries, when 160 mosques and madrasas were established in Damascus, 26 of which were funded by women through the Wakf system. Half of all the royal patrons for these institutions were also women. According to the Sunni scholar Ibn Asakir, in the 12th century, there were various opportunities for female education in what is popularly known as the 'medieval Islamic world'. He writes that women could study, earn ijazahs (academic degrees), and qualify as ulema (scholars) and teachers. This was especially the case for learned and scholarly families, who wanted to ensure the highest possible education for both their sons and daughters. Ibn Asakir had himself studied under 80 different female teachers in his time.

Female education in the Islamic world was inspired by Muhammad's wives: Khadijah, a successful businesswoman, and Aisha, a renowned hadith scholar and military leader. However, in many cases, education allowed was often restricted to religious instruction. According to a hadith attributed to Muhammad, he praised the women of Medina because of their desire for religious knowledge.

According to the 2010 Census, there were over 70 million Muslim women in India. In popular perception Muslim women are often seen as covered and cloistered, hidden from view. The spotlight, when it falls on them, tends to do no more than view the role of religion in their lives and reinforce the usual stereotypes: purdah, multiple marriages, triple talaq, etc., the male privilege of unilateral divorce amongst others.

The truth, however, is that like women from other communities, Indian-Muslim women too are differentiated across class, caste, community, and geographical location, including the great rural-urban divide. However, even compared to women from other faiths in India, the majority of Indian-Muslim women are among the most disadvantaged, least literate, most economically impoverished, and politically marginalized sections of Indian society.

The great tragedy is that most Indian-Muslim women are often seen, within and without the community, as a group who are less than equally entitled to the same rights that the Constitution of India grants to all its citizens. The right to education, especially at the primary level is mandated by the Constitution, yet after 73 years of Independence less than 50% of Muslim women in India are literate. Compare this with other women from other minorities: 76% literacy among Christians, 64% among Sikhs, 62% among Buddhists, and a whopping 90% among Jain women.[28]

According to an ORG-Marg Muslim Women's survey—commissioned by the Nehru Memorial Museum and Library, New Delhi—conducted in 2000-2001 in 40 districts spanning 12 states, the enrolment percentage of Indian-Muslim girl children is a mere 40.66%. As a consequence, the proportion of Indian-Muslim women in higher education is a mere 3.56%. In comparison scheduled castes have a higher percentage at 4.25%. On an all-India basis, 66% Indian-Muslim women are stated to be illiterate.[29]

The illiteracy is most widespread in Haryana while

Kerala has the least illiteracy among Muslim women closely followed by Tamil Nadu. Muslim women are found to be more literate than their Hindu counterparts in the states of Madhya Pradesh, Maharashtra, Andhra Pradesh, Karnataka, and Tamil Nadu. Most of the northern states are in urgent need of vigorous and sustained literacy campaigns.

Muslim women have played an important and historic role as scholars and leaders in education. Apart from Princess Fatima Al-Fihri during the Ayyubid dynasty, the regent queen Dafiya Khatun built numerous khanqas (Sufi convents) and madrasas in Damascus and Aleppo. Thus, given equal opportunity, Muslim women worldwide would excel. The names of Zahabiya Khorakiwala of Wockhardt Group come to my mind as one example of successful Indian-Muslim businesswoman.

The growing hunger for education and opportunity amongst girls and women from all community, including the Muslim community can no longer be ignored. Women themselves have come together to create self-help and other initiatives when they feel the State or society has been ignoring their demands and aspirations. One such example is the Minorities Vikas Manch in Jaipur that is doing phenomenal work to raise Indian-Muslim women's literacy level in Rajasthan.

Elsewhere, private educational institutions have stepped in providing both secular and religious education. Another such example is Anwar-ul-Ulum Women's Arabic College which was established in 1966 in the village of

Mongam near Calicut. They provide education in a blend of modern and Islamic education, working with the Meo of Haryana Lok Jumbish (People's Movement), an NGO specializing in education. Lok Jumbish found a simple but workable solution to increase literacy level from a low of 10% simply by providing modern education in Urdu thereby circumventing the community elders' concerns.

The link between poverty and illiteracy among Muslim women cannot be over-emphasised. Regardless of whether illiteracy is a consequence of poverty or vice versa what Muslim women want today is some form of knowledge that empowers them to improve their condition in an increasingly knowledge-driven world. The government's madrasa-modernisation scheme or political promise of 'Education for All' amount to little if the incentives fail to trickle down to the target—in this case the Indian-Muslim women.

It is just not the issue of providing education, the quality of education is just as important. It has been seen that after the first few years of the primary education afforded to the Indian-Muslim girl child, the student is plucked out of formal education to assist in everyday activities or worse for marriage and for all practical purposes lapses into virtual illiteracy.

In the second scenario, if by good fortune she still continues in school, with every year the quality of education available to her is so inferior that it equips her for very little. For all effect, by the time she graduates she is nothing more than an 'uneducated literate'. The quality of education, along with the competency of instruction by the teachers in some Urdu-medium schools is so inadequate that the girls who do come out from such institutions—many privately run, others with dubious affiliations from quasi-religious bodies—can not cope in a competitive environment.

The famous saying, 'Educate a man and you educate an individual, educate a woman and you educate a family', applies very well in the Indian context, more so in the context of Indian-Muslim women, a large section of whom have been denied education for a variety of reasons either rooted in government apathy or poor understanding of the religion.

Historically, while there has always been a gap between the education of boys and girls in India, in the case of Muslims, the gap has been a yawning chasm. The education of girls has always demanded higher investment in terms of more facilities, more women teachers, separate schools, transport, and scholarships to provide the much-needed incentives. Despite pressures of religious orthodoxies, social prejudice and class/gender bias, Indian-Muslim women at the start of the 20th century successfully emerged from the isolation of traditional roles as self aware individuals, determined to claim a greater role in public affairs. In today's modern and progressive India, Muslim women should come out openly against any inequalities and discriminations aimed against them and fight and claim their rights courageously.

We must encourage them to achieve their dreams,

not give them up. I feel extraordinarily proud of my three extremely talented daughters who not only distinguished themselves in their education but have also proved to be successful entrepreneurs: Farah Ali Khan (Farah Khan Jewels, worldwide respected brand and clientele), Simone Arora (D'décor, world's largest home décor brand, and AD x Simone) and Sussanne Khan (The Charcoal Project, leading interiors store) have attained world-wide respect and name for their respective achievements.

SECTION V

INDIAN-MUSLIM ENTREPRENEURSHIP & LEADERSHIP

*'The ink from a scholar's pen is far mightier than
the blood of a thousand martyrs.'*
- Prophet Mohammad (MPBUH)

As India rises and takes its rightful place in the 21st century world order, it is with pride that we take the name of various Indian brands that have gone global. Companies like Tata, which purchased and turned around iconic British brands like Jaguar and Land Rover, or multinationals like Reliance and TCS, Infosys amongst others. But except for Wipro and Cipla, headed by Azim Premji and Hamid Yusuf, none of the global brands from India seem to be headed by an Indian-Muslim, with the exception the Kerala Muslims like Yusuf Ali, who is the owner of a large chain of shopping mall in the Gulf countries and has also part-funded the Trivandrum airport. The

Tamil Muslims in Tamil Nadu are leading merchants in the leather business. It is believed that in the leather centre called Mallamwadi, the final trading quotes for leather are made.

It is with great satisfaction and pride I draw from the following stories and achievements of these wonderful and courageous Indian-Muslims whose inspirational force and entrepreneurship in running businesses with considerable initiative and risk, to achieve the targeted goals, is truly inspiring. Though there are many mid-level businesses run by Indian-Muslims, on the global scale there are few who have achieved amazing success.

AZIM PREMJI
CHAIRMAN, WIPRO INDUSTRIES

Azim Premji was born in Bombay, India, in a Nizari Ismaili Shia Muslim family with origins from Kutch in Gujarat. His father was a noted businessman and was known as the 'Rice King of Burma'. After the Partition, when Jinnah invited his father Muhammed Hashem Premji to come to Pakistan, he turned down the request and chose to remain in India.

Premji has been recognized by *Business Week* as one of the *Greatest Entrepreneurs* for being responsible for Wipro emerging as one of the world's fastest-growing companies.

In 2000, he was conferred an honorary doctorate by the Manipal Academy of Higher Education. In 2006,

Azim Premji was awarded Lakshya Business Visionary by National Institute of Industrial Engineering, Mumbai. In 2009, he was awarded an honorary doctorate from Wesleyan University in Middletown, Connecticut, for his outstanding philanthropic work. In 2015, Mysore University conferred an honorary doctorate on him.

In 2005, the Government of India honoured him with the title of Padma Bhushan for his outstanding work in trade and commerce. In 2011, he was awarded Padma Vibhushan, the second-highest civilian award by the Government of India. In April 2017, *India Today* magazine ranked him 9th in India's 50 Most powerful people of 2017 list.

In 2001, he founded Azim Premji Foundation, a non-profit organization. In December 2010, he pledged to donate USD 2 billion for improving school education in India. This has been done by transferring 213 million equity shares of Wipro Ltd., held by a few entities controlled by him, to the Azim Premji Trust. This donation is the largest of its kind in India. In March 2019, Premji pledged an additional 34% of Wipro stock held by him to the foundation. At a current value of about USD 7.5 billion, this allocation will bring the total endowment from him to the foundation to USD 21 billion.

Premji has said that being rich 'did not thrill' him. He became the first Indian to sign up for The Giving Pledge, a campaign led by Warren Buffett and Bill Gates, to encourage the wealthiest people to make a commitment to give most of their wealth to philanthropic causes. He is the third non-American after Richard Branson and David Sainsbury to join this philanthropy club.

DR YUSUF K HAMIED
CHAIRMAN, CIPLA LTD.

Dr Yusuf K Hamied was born in Vilnius, Lithuania, and raised in Bombay. His north Indian Muslim father and Russophone Lithuanian Jewish mother met in pre-war Berlin, where they were university students. Hamied was educated at the Cathedral and John Connon School and St Xavier's College, Mumbai. He later went to England and earned a PhD in chemistry from Christ's College, Cambridge. He uses his chemistry notebooks from Cambridge when he develops new syntheses of drugs.

Hamied is best known outside India for defying large Western pharmaceutical companies in order to provide generic AIDS drugs and treatments for other ailments primarily affecting people in poor countries. Hamied has led efforts to eradicate AIDS in the developing world and to give patients life-saving medicines regardless of their ability to pay and has been characterized as a modern-day Robin Hood figure as a result.

Hamied stated, "I don't want to make money off these diseases which cause the whole fabric of society to crumble."

In September 2011, in a piece about how he was trying to radically lower costs of biotech drugs for cancer, diabetes, and other non-communicable diseases, *The New York Times* wrote of Hamied: 'Dr Yusuf K Hamied, chairman of the Indian drug giant Cipla Ltd., electrified the global health community a decade ago when he said he could produce cocktails of AIDS medicines for $1 per day—a fraction of the price charged by branded pharmaceutical companies. That price has since fallen to 20 cents per day, and more than six million people in the developing world now receive treatment, up from little more than 2,000 in 2001.'

Hamied has also been influential in pioneering development of multi-drug combination pills (also known as fixed-dose combinations, or FDCs), notably for HIV/AIDS, tuberculosis (TB), asthma and other ailments chiefly affecting developing countries, as well as development of paediatric formulations of drugs, especially those benefiting children in poor settings. These innovations have greatly expanded access to medicine and increased drug safety by ensuring proper dosages are taken. He is also highly regarded for his role in expanding the production of bulk drugs and 'active pharmaceutical ingredients' (APIs, the active chemical components in medicines) in India.

In 2009, the Yusuf Hamied Centre was opened at Christ's College, Cambridge. The centre features a bronze portrait bust of Hamied by fellow Christ's College alumnus, Anthony Smith.

Hamied has been the subject of in-depth profiles in *The New York Times*, *Time* magazine, *The Guardian*, *Le Monde*, *The Economist*, the *Financial Times*, *The Times (London)*, *Corriere della Sera*, *Der Spiegel*, *Wired*, and numerous other leading publications, as well as on television outlets such as *ABC News*, the BBC, CNN and CBS' *60 Minutes*.

In February 2013, Hamied announced his retirement plans from Cipla after remaining managing director of the company for 52 years. That year *Forbes* magazine included him in its list of richest Indians.

Hamied's role in the battle for mass antiretroviral treatment in Africa is portrayed in the documentary *Fire in the Blood*. In its review of the film, *India Today* noted that 'the story of Yusuf Hamied will make every Indian proud as he was the only man who decided to walk against the tide and sell drugs to save lives without focusing on profits'.

DR HABIL KHORAKIWALA
CHAIRMAN, WOCKHARDT GROUP

The Wockhardt group is the first true healthcare group from India, and Dr Habil Khorakiwala has been the captain of this ship. Dr Khorakiwala majored in Pharmacy from LM College in Ahmedabad and later acquired a master's degree in pharmaceutical science from Purdue University. He was the only international non-American to have been given the title of 'Distinguished Aluminous' by Purdue University. Thereafter he studied in an Advanced Management Programme at the Harvard Business School in Boston.

He returned to India and took over what was a small firm that made OTC (Over-The-Counter) medications. It has now blossomed into a giant multi-national company making him a pharma tycoon in its true sense. As of today, Wockhardt is a USD 841 million (and counting) pharmaceutical company. The firm engages in an endless list of CSR activities and has a workforce of 7500 people from 14 nations. The Government of India has nominated Dr Habil Khorakiwala for various committees and councils. He is quite the family man, and an avid reader and philanthropist.

YUSUFF ALI MA
CHAIRMAN, LULU GROUP

Yusuff Ali MA is a UAE based Indian billionaire, businessman, and Padma Shri award winner from Nattika, Thrissur district, Kerala. He is the chairman and managing director of LuLu Group International that owns the Lulu Hypermarket chain worldwide and LuLu International Shopping Mall. With an annual turnover of USD 7.4 billion globally, LuLu Group International employs the largest number of Indians outside India. According to *Forbes*, Yusuff Ali was ranked the 21st wealthiest Indian and the 270th (as of 2018) richest in the world, with a personal wealth of USD 5.2 billion. According to *Forbes Middle East*, Yusuff Ali was ranked No. 1 in Top 100 Indian Business Owners in the Arab World in 2018. In 2013, Yusuff Ali acquired 4.99% equity in the 93-year-old Thrissur-based Catholic Syrian Bank (CSB) and increased his stake in the Aluva-based Federal Bank to 4.47%. In 2016, Yusuff Ali purchased the Scotland Yard Building in London. As of 2013, he holds a 9.37% share in Cochin International Airport. He has bought a 10% stake in the UK-based trading firm, East India Company, and a 40% stake in its fine foods subsidiary for around $85 million in total. Lulu's project of Lulu Bolgatty International Convention Centre in Bolgatty Island is one of the largest convention centres in South Asia along with the third-largest Grand Hyatt branded hotel in the same campus.

Yusuff Ali is very closely involved in many social, charitable and humanitarian activities both in India as well as in the Arab states of the Gulf. He has done various philanthropic activities across the globe. As part of its Global CSR policy, the Lulu Group joined hands with Dubai Cares and adopted schools in Gaza and Nepal. Yusuff Ali contributed and took initiative to open a multi-faith funeral centre for the Indian community in Sharjah that spread across 8.3 acres. He also took the initiative to sell and promote organic products grown by the special needs community in UAE through Lulu Hypermarkets. He is also actively involved in ensuring the social, economic, and religious welfare of expatriate Indians in the Persian Gulf region. He played a major role in finding land for the Christian community in the region to build churches and secure cremation grounds for the Hindu populace in the Gulf region. Yusuff Ali also extended help to Indians during the amnesty period in the Persian Gulf when hundreds of Indians lost their livelihood. He helped rehabilitate people who lost their livelihood in the Calicut market fire as well. He has pledged to donate of INR 50 million (Dh2.5 million) for the flood-hit south Indian state of Kerala in the event of the 2019 Kerala floods.

AYAZ BASRAI
FOUNDER, THE BUSRIDE

The dream of an idea is often sweeter than its reality. Not so much for Ayaz Basrai. A pass-out of the National Institute of Design (Ahmedabad), Ayaz graduated in industrial design and specialized in product design.

After working in studios like Ideaspice Design Studio (Dubai), Lokus Design, and XHeight Design studio, he moved on and founded The Busride, an independent design studio, which seems to have touched almost every field you could think of: office spaces (Sony music studio, Channel V studio), retail spaces (The Shantanu Nikhil Gallery, The Turtle Retail Stores), houses (one at Ranwar and one at Tutikorin), and even films (*Krrish*, *Chandni Chowk to China*). Apart from Busride, Ayaz also runs The Gypsy Kitchen. He is passionate about Bandra and organizes Bandra Walks.

AZHAR IQUBAL
CO-FOUNDER & CEO, INSHORTS

Today everyone is busy. Either they are busy with work or in their daily chores. Seldom people make time to read the news. But it's essential for everybody to stay updated about the happenings in and around the world. Wouldn't it be amazing if the news were filtered and shortened for you? Azhar Iqubal, an IIT Delhi dropout, started up with News in Shorts (formerly called) along with Anunay Arunav of IIT Delhi and Deepit Purkayastha of IIT Kharagpur in 2013.

This young entrepreneur has turned our dreams into a reality by creating the app, Inshorts. The app provides an experience of knowing it all without reading it all. The app curates news from all the sources, handpicks the best articles, and provides the gist of those stories in just 60 words.

FARHAN AZMI
CEO, INFINITY HOTELS PVT. LTD.

There are places you don't want to be put in, and then there are places you do. Farhan Azmi gives you the latter. The politician-cum-hotelier finished his schooling at The Scholar High School and studied commerce at Jai Hind and Sydenham College.

What started as a hangout place for friends has metamorphosed into Infinity Hotels Pvt. Ltd., which is the parent company of Koyla, Café Basilico, Basilico House, and ChaiCoffi. Each is unique in its concept and the audience it looks to serve. All throughout, Farhan has carefully carved himself a niche, keeping in mind what he calls the 'space-starved' Mumbaikars. Farhan evidently has grand expansion plans for Infinity Hotels and he's juggling politics and business well.

FAISAL FAROOQUI
FOUNDER & CEO, MOUTHSHUT.COM
AND DEALFACE.COM

Want to talk tirelessly? Talk Faisal Farooqui. Faisal graduated as a Bachelor in Science as well as in Finance from The State University of New York, Binghamton. He, unlike many in his stead, returned to India after the completion of his course and founded mouthshut.com, an online customer feedback and interaction portal. As of now, it has recorded over six million users a month and counting.

Faisal also co-founded Zarca Interactive, an online survey software. He has received various awards and titles, like the Manthan Award by the Government of India, Best Youth Website (2006), Indian Digital Media Awards: Best Web Portal of the Year-Gold (2011), etc. In addition to the awards, he was named Top Entrepreneur by the *Entrepreneur* magazine in 2012 and one of the Top 100 Digital Icons of India 2012. When he isn't busy receiving awards, he's giving talks at prestigious institutions such as the American University in Dubai, IIM Ahmedabad, and IIT Mumbai. He authored 'Application of Market Research Towards Proactive Customer Relationship Management' in 2003. What's more, he has also pioneered auto rickshaw advertising.

GULREZ ALAM
GLOBAL COO, RESULTRIX

Social media and e-commerce are essential weapons for the success and sustenance of companies. Without SEO and SEM, they would be as good as a gun without bullets. Gulrez Alam has spent more than a decade of making social media and e-commerce useful to his clients.

Gulrez, an MBA from IILM, New Delhi, founded Resultrix in 2008. It is a leading service provider of search engine marketing (SEM), search engine optimization (SEO), affiliate, and social media marketing. They are certified partners with Google AdWords and Google Analytics. Resultrix has also been listed as a Microsoft adExcellence Company. In a matter of six years of its formation, it has been acquired by Publicis Group. If you do want to catch him while he's in Mumbai and make it look accidental, try the Sunday Farmer's Market at Bandra.

IRFAN ALAM
FOUNDER, SAMMAN

Irfan Alam was fond of comics as a child and is now an entrepreneurial superhero for over five million rickshaw operators. As a twelve-year-old, Irfan studied the stock market and helped his father make investment decisions. By the age of fifteen, he launched Matins, a portfolio management firm that managed over Indian INR 60 lakhs (nearly USD 14,000). As an older man, the Harvard graduate identified an opportunity that would ease out the life for rickshaw operators as well as their clients and carried extensive research for the same at IIM Ahmedabad. In 2006, he participated in a competition announced by a television channel for entrepreneurs to showcase their business ideas. He won the contest and was titled 'Business Baazigar'.

Irfan declined to accept the investment, in a very hero-like move, over the investors' demands of the firm being for-profit and their demand to hold a majority of stakes in it. He structured a model that ensured that he and the community (with the community owning a majority) will together hold at least 51% of the stakes in Samman, which organized the most scattered income generating sector in India—the rickshaw operators. It doesn't stop there. The rickshaws that are part of Samman are also a selling point for various products and services. The rickshaw operators and their families have been made 'full economic citizens' by Irfan's efforts to build channels for essential services such as banking, individual access to credit, and health for them. He was invited for Presidential Summit, 2010, at Washington by US President Barack Obama. He has won himself various titles and awards. All he needs now is a cape!

IRFAN RAZACK
MANAGING DIRECTOR, PRESTIGE GROUP

Bread, clothing, and shelter are our basic needs. The Razack Sattar family deals in the latter two. Irfan Razack is Mr Sattar's eldest son. He studied commerce and graduated from St Joseph's College (Bangalore University) and was also awarded the Lifetime Achievement Award by St. Joseph's Old Boys Association. Later on, he completed a course in Jordan by the United Nations University International's Leadership Academy (UNU/ILA).

Irfan established Prestige in 1986, which is now a public company, with over 90 million square feet of commercial, retail, and residential properties gracing its profile so far. His love for extreme adventure is reflected in the goals he sets for Prestige and the velocity at which the company is expanding. He guided it for INR 4300 crore, which amounts to about 8 million square feet for the financial year 2014. Mr Sattar has received many awards, including Real Estate Excellence Award (2008) and the Best Developer Award (2009) by Karnataka State Town Planning Development. He has also held important posts like Honorary secretary of Al-Ameen Educational Society,

President of Bangalore Commercial Association (BCA), and Chairman of CREDAI.

JAVED AKHTAR
CEO, TRAVELPORT

The obvious direct relationship between employee productivity and employee satisfaction demands that corporates give as much attention to their internal audience as they do to their external audience. Javed Akhtar, a graduate from St Georges College, Heena JA, and Bhavin Parekh witnessed the plight of these corporates and identified the tremendous opportunity that comes with it. They fit together all the elements of loyalty and promotions programs, and Travelport was born.

They started off in a small office at Dharavi in 2002. Twelve years on, they have expanded and ventured into the rewards and recognition programs as well. Rewardport, as they call it, serves over 250 clients with a team of 150 professionals, with a turnover of over INR 100 crore. This taste of success seems to have made Javed crave for more! Already having covered a strong market share in both corporate travel plans and corporate reward plans, he's now tapping the potential in the travel market for non-corporate individuals. Javed has also come up with the idea of opening travel offices in malls, adding convenience to quality.

JAWED HABIB
MANAGING DIRECTOR, JHHBL

Jawed's grandfather, Nazir Ahmed, cut the hair of almost all the heavyweights among Indian and British politicians of the likes of Jawaharlal Nehru and Lord Mountbatten. Jawed, a graduate in French literature from Jawaharlal Nehru University, is undoubtedly romantic, but for hairdressing! He completed a nine-month hairdressing course at Morris International School in London post his graduation. Soon after he was hired by Sunsilk and he gave the firm a good nine years of service before returning to India.

Here in India, Jawed started units in remote places and trained a handful of students at a time. The trained students were then encouraged to go back to their hometown and gather a group of five people for his lecture. Then he'd start a salon with them! This soon formed a chain. Today, JHHBL has 207 saloons and 41 academies across India, and one in Malaysia. He now intends to diversify and offer his clients all that is related to haircare and beauty. Shampoos, serums, cosmetics, hair clips, razors, spas, (salon) chairs, cups, electronic hair appliances, you name it and it's on his mind already.

JAZEEL BADUR FERRY
CO-FOUNDER, EVENTIFIER

"Never let success get into your head and never let your failure get to your heart." These are the wise words dominating Jazeel's Facebook page cover photo. The 23-year-old completed an undergraduate degree in computer science and engineering from Mangalore. He and his friends failed at impressing the jury of The Startup Centre hackathon with their idea to build an app related to stock market integrating the SMS feature.

A year later, though, they floored the jury with their idea of Eventifier, which was born out of a seemingly casual observation that there was no online portal to archive the pictures and social media discussions threads that were formed while the event was on. Eventifier's incubation at The Startup Centre hackathon was the starting point of the ride the three friends were getting onto. It was listed as one of the seven most interesting social media start-ups at the Web Summit, Ireland. The start-up has now been funded with USD 5,00,000 by Accel Partners and Kae Capital.

MOHAMMED HISAMUDDIN
CO-FOUNDER, INNOZ TECH & QUEST

While the world is busy going gaga over the internet, Mohammed and two of his friends were busy unlocking the treasures of SMS apps. Mohammed graduated from

Lal Bahadur Shastri College of Engineering, Kerala. The idea of Innoz was formed in a hostel room while the start-up itself was jointly incubated at IIM Ahmedabad and Technopark Trivandrum.

Quest is an Android and iOS based application that functions as a search engine where people answer questions posed by other people. Innoz has been recorded as the largest offline search engine, 2013, in the Limca Book of Records. It has also won a number of awards, including Nasscom Top 8 Emerging Technology Companies in India 2010, Top 10 Mobile Application Developers in India 2010, and Top 10 Emerging Product Companies 2011. In addition, they won MIT-TR35 for 2010 and were shortlisted for the GSMA Global Mobile Awards 2012. Mohammed Hisamuddin follows football, cricket, and tennis and likes to read non-fiction books. With so many things on his plate, we wonder where he gets all the time for it.

NAVAJ SHARIEF
FOUNDER, AMMI'S BIRYANI

What's better than a traditional homemade biryani? A traditional homemade biryani packed in a box and delivered to you! Meet the guy who brought this about: Navaj Sharief. He completed his schooling from Baldwin Boys High School and moved on to pursue his BBA and MBA from the Bangalore University. Navaj left the comfort of a well-established, family-owned business to start Ammi's Biryani in 2008.

He believes in building the city before building the fort. It comes as no surprise, then, that he single-handedly built the company from scratch first, transcending from one role to another whenever required. The building of a strong management and HR team around it came later, with stabilization. This strategy has worked wonders for him. Today, Ammi's Biryani has over 30 outlets spread across Bangalore and Chennai. It has been applauded for its flawless packaging and its appealing quality of food on various blogs. Navaj bagged the Best Entrepreneur Award at the Maeeshat Awards ceremony, 2013.

SHAHNAZ HUSAIN
FOUNDER, SHAHNAZ HUSAIN GROUP

If sheer grit and independence could be a woman, it would be Shahnaz Husain. She was schooled at La Martiniere, Lucknow, and was married by the tender age of 15. Shahnaz accompanied her husband to his posting in Tehran. There, beauty treatments intrigued her more than ever and she made up her mind to study cosmetology. Driven by her will to be independent, she supported her education by writing articles for the *Iran Tribune*. She worked with some of the leading institutions in the world, like Schwarzkopf, Helena Rubinstein, Lancôme, Christine Valmy, and Lean of Copenhagen. The occurrences of chemical damage due to beauty treatments inspired her to look for a safer, more dependable alternative.

She found Ayurveda, and there was no looking back. Now a mother, she started her business in the comfort of her home, with an initial investment of INR 35,000 from her father. Soon, she was elected Chairman of the ITEC International Beauty Congress in 1981 and later in the year represented India at the Cosmetics Fair at Brighton, UK. The sale of her products broke the cosmetics sales record at Selfridges, and there was no looking back after. As of today, Shahnaz Husain has expanded her business to over 100 countries, branching into various segments like salons, spas, and shops.

SYED MOHAMMED BEARY
CMD, BEARY'S GROUP

Syed Mohammed Beary started off as a real estate consultant in 1981. Within three decades, Beary's Group grew into a giant empire, offering solutions for everything, from design, development, construction, management, coordination to marketing and advisory services. Today, Beary's is involved in total reality, property development, and turnkey solutions, infrastructure and construction engineering, shariah as well as education.

Syed spent his childhood in the picturesque hilly region of Chikmagalur. His love for nature forms an integral part of all the projects his group takes up. The entire Beary's

Group is supported on three pillars: entrepreneurship, environment, and education. The BGRT is India's first sustainable green building research park. They have as many as 16 educational institutes across the coastal towns of Karnataka. The group has won multiple awards over the years.

SIRAJUDDIN QURESHI
CMD, HIND INDUSTRIES

Sirajuddin Qureshi was born an entrepreneur. As a child, he supported his education by buying small goods and selling them on the roadside. He graduated from University of Delhi and pursued Law after. Hind Industries saw its inception with Mr Qureshi's first consignment—an order of meat worth Rs. 17,000 to Dubai. Today, Hind Industries has its presence in 50 countries, with interests in agro-processing, abattoirs, livestock development, engineering, education, hospitality, and power. In 2010, Sirajuddin Qureshi was invited by US President Barack Obama for an entrepreneurial summit in Washington.

Mr Qureshi is also president of the Indian Islamic Culture Centre. Having realized the importance of education very early on in life, Mr Qureshi has taken upon himself to help scores of youngsters from the minority sections of the society and educated them through the Noble Education Foundation of IICC. He also bears all the expenses towards the education provided. Mr Qureshi has been honoured with several awards and recognitions from the Government of India for his contributions to the export industry.

ZOHER KHORAKIWALA
CHAIRMAN, MONGINIS

In the times when cakes were a luxury affordable only to the highest class, Monginis gave the common man reason to 'Go ahead, celebrate!'. Zoher Khorakiwala grew up to a constant cycle of wooden trays filled with fresh cakes and puffs entering the bakery and getting exhausted within minutes. He joined the family business in 1972. Since then much has changed and much has stayed the same. The cake shop of the common man has adapted itself to local tastes as it built franchises all over the world. The evergreen favourites like the black forest cake and the pineapple pastry, though, have remained untouched.

Monginis has kept up with the dynamic technological advancements, entering into e-commerce and even offering varieties like 'photo' cakes. Not to forget the packaged moist cakes have gained popularity. Zoher Khorakiwala has strategized the expansion of Monginis in such a way that they consolidate their presence in the places where they already have stores. We think these are grand, deserving plans. After all, who hasn't heard of Monginis?

ZARINE KHAN
FOUNDER, TRADITION
AUTHOR, *FAMILY SECRETS*

Zarine Khan has created an identity of her own in the world of interiors for the past four decades. She has clients across the world and has designed homes of royalty and movie stars and also designed corporates and five-star hotels.

She also brought out a cookbook, *Family Secrets: The Khan Family Cookbook*, which won the top award in 'Best in the World in the Entertainment Food' category from the highly prestigious World Gourmand Awards in 2016. She also hosts the highly appreciated cookery show on Living Foodz through Zee Channel called *Spices & Secrets*.

In this spirit, we can truly call Mrs Zarine Khan a woman of empowerment and a lady of substance.

FARAH KHAN ALI
FOUNDER, FARAH KHAN FINE JEWELLERY

With over two decades of experience, Farah Khan is not just a jewellery designer but an artist of masterpieces and an orator of stories. Her creations are conceived in her fecund imagination that allows her the freedom to make the impossible possible and her tales of thought, inspiration, and craftsmanship is narrated within her bejewelled jewellery theatre.

Artiste, style icon, and art lover, a philanthropist, both dancer and athlete, mother and fashionista, a digital influencer, Farah is inspirational for all those who follow her lifestyle as she effortlessly balances her personal and her professional life. To mark 25 years of her career and 15 years of her eponymous brand *Farah Khan*, she launched a coffee table book *Farah Khan – A Bejewelled Life* across 70 different countries.

From being featured on many magazine covers including *Forbes India Marquee* to being named as one of the most powerful women in Indian luxury, Farah has also been featured in a UK-based digital algorithm on twitter as one of the world's topmost 250 influencers, among other prominent women like Hillary Clinton and Oprah Winfrey.

From music icon Beyoncé and tennis star Serena Williams to A-list Hollywood and Bollywood celebrities, the biggest names in the business have worn her jewellery on the most photographed international red carpets.

Winner of many prestigious awards and accolades that range from her professional achievements to 'Outstanding Women Achiever's Awards' and 'Woman Of Substance Awards', Farah epitomises the modern woman of today. one that is courageous and strong, one that supports social causes to make a difference in someone's life, one that stands up to what she believes in, and one who multitasks all her roles with great ease.

SUSSANNE KHAN
FOUNDER, THE CHARCOAL PROJECT

Sussanne Khan obtained an associate art degree in interior design from Brooks College, Long Beach, California, in the year 1995, and went on to design her first project in 1996. She is the founder and the heart and mind behind The Charcoal Project, India's first and most unique design concept store. The store changed the meaning of curated interior design in India. Meticulously created by Sussanne herself, the store has two commanding levels and presents lines by premier global and Indian designers Andrew Martin, Abu Jani & Sandeep Khosla, and her very own hand-crafted furniture collection Sussanne Khan prét home. She uses metal, wood, natural fibres, concrete, geometric patterns, organic forms, embellishments, all subtly woven together to create what she calls quite luxe, her signature style which is a seamless blend of industrial masculine with feminine edgy chic. Her belief is that luxury is about emotion and design is her tool.

At the Charcoal Project, Sussanne has delivered many conceptual projects in the world of residential, private homes, destination villas, commercial offices and model show apartments for various leading real estate brands.

SIMONE ARORA
FOUNDER, DESIGNER, AND CURATOR

For over two decades, Simone Arora has been the creative force behind the designs of D'Decor, India's leading home furnishing brand, and the founder, curator, and designer of SIMONE, a luxury home decor store based in South Mumbai.

Simone is an avid traveller with a keen eye for detail and finds creative inspiration in the beauty and textures of nature. Her signature decor style is sophisticated and elegant, understated yet luxurious. With all her talent, travel experience and eclectic design sensibilities, Simone has dressed the homes of some of India's biggest celebrity names in the corporate and film industry.

ZAYED KHAN
FOUNDER, HUNGRY WOLVES ENTERTAINMENT

A business management graduate from the Montgomery College, Washington DC, and having thereafter studied film making at London Film School, Zayed is a Bollywood actor who has acted in movies like *Chura Liya Hai Tumne*, *Main Hoon Na*, *Shabd*, *Dus*, *Yuvraaj*, *Blue*, and *Anjaana Anjaani*.

Besides acting, Zayed has assisted his father in the construction of a super deluxe 5-star hotel, The Golden Palms and Spa, in Bangalore. And also helped initiate an ambitious '7 Cities Project' at Agra on the creatives.

He currently pours his passion and time in his film production company, Hungry Wolves Entertainment, aimed at creating content for the emerging markets.

***

Besides the people that have been profiled, there is a huge macrocosm of people out there who have been doing outstanding work, serving society without any material gain regardless of caste, creed, and religion. They understand the human element, the human cause, and the human spirit, which prompts them to take the path of altruism. It gives me deep satisfaction in communicating to the world their selfless contributions and magnanimous concerns for the betterment of society. A healthy vibrant society makes a strong vibrant nation.

MOHD SUJATHULLAH
FOUNDER, HUMANITY FIRST

Mohd Sujathullah wakes up early and leaves his house around 7:30 every morning. He reaches Koti Maternity Hospital in Hyderabad, where three hundred poor patients have already queued up and are waiting for a meal. Within fifteen minutes, he, along with a volunteer or two, finishes distributing hot raw upma to them and proceeds to his next destination—Nilofer Children's Hospital. There, about seven hundred people are waiting to get their own bowl of breakfast after spending a restless night on the grounds of this government hospital.

Mohd Sujathullah, a Pharmacy student from India, distributes free food to people every day and has founded a NGO named Humanity First in Hyderabad.

For the past many years he has been sticking to a daily routine of feeding breakfast to around thousand people and then sitting down to eat his own.

An average student at school who had learning difficulties early on, Sujathullah went on to pursue a Bachelor's in Pharmacy from Sultan Ul Uloom College, Hyderabad. Sujathullah was raised in a joint family of twenty-five members and he grew up experiencing the joy of sharing. But the true happiness one can derive from sharing, especially with the lesser privileged, did not hit him until the day he vowed to feed ten people if he passed a college exam.

He then returned to his house and convinced his family to dedicate one day's earnings in a month for this cause. Seeing passion and determination in his cause, his family came forward to help him start distributing food three to four times a week to around hundred and fifty people.

With a daily expense of INR 3,500, he now feeds between seven hundred to a thousand people every day in the streets around the hospital. During the summers, Sujathullah organizes frequent water camps, and in winters conducts blanket distribution drives.

In 2016 Sujathullah established the non-profit organization Humanity First Foundation Hyderabad and initiated new projects alongside his free food drives. The most remarkable one is Project Transformation, an initiative to transform the lives of the homeless. The Project helps homeless people reform their lives and provides the support needed for their makeover and rehabilitation. With the support of donors and volunteers, they also conduct regular medical camps at slums and distribute free medicines post-check-ups. Visits to orphanages and ration distribution are other activities undertaken by the organization to promote social welfare in and around areas of Hyderabad. Undeterred by the obstacles, Sujathullah stands tall in his conviction and sets a good example for the millennials to rise above the everyday challenges and selflessly serve those in need.

SYED GULAB
FOUNDER, GULAB'S ROTI CHARITY TRUST

Bengaluru's Syed Gulab sure has a big heart, but he is nowhere close to being financially rich, and that is what makes his efforts all the more remarkable. Gulab, a 39-year-old former wall painter, and now a motor vehicle insurance agent, runs a one-of-a-kind free food campaign in front of Rajiv Gandhi Institute of TB and Chest Diseases in Someshwara Nagar, Bengaluru, and feeds close to two hundred needy people every day.

Gulab got the idea to start the campaign when his niece was admitted to a hospital and the child's poor parents would remain without food for days, due to lack of money. Gulab witnessed similar instances with other poor families during his visit to the hospital and felt a desire to do something about it.

It was tough initially because he barely had money to feed his three children, but he persevered. Today, Gulab's Roti Charity Trust serves close to two hundred people every day, earning praise from all quarters. The trust has employed a full-time cook. The cook's salary of INR 7,500 per month is managed by the donations the organization receives. At a recent event to mark the first anniversary of his campaign, Dr Shashidhar Buggi, Director of Rajiv Gandhi Institute of TB and Chest Diseases, offered to become a trustee of the organization, and extended his wholehearted support. Gulab says it's a shame that millions of people go hungry every day, while most people throw away the leftover food. "My team and I have taken a small step in tackling this issue. Hopefully, it will have an impact," he says.

AZHAR MAQSUSI
FOUNDER, SANI WELFARE TRUST

Azhar Maqsusi is the founder of the Sani Welfare Association, a non-profitable trust based out of Hyderabad. Growing up, Azhar's family didn't have a lot of money, and on many nights he would have to go to bed on an empty stomach. When he was eight years old, he promised himself that one day he'd do whatever he could to alleviate hunger for the poor.

He started realizing his dream in 2012, when he first distributed free food at Dabeerpura, Hyderabad. Now, his initiative has extended to cities like Bengaluru, Raichur, Tandur and even into the states of Jharkhand and Assam. His free food distribution program offers a nutritious meal to around thousand to twelve hundred people daily.

AFROZ SHAH
ENVIRONMENTAL ORGANIZER; AMBASSADOR, CHAMPIONS OF THE EARTH FOUNDATION, UNITED NATION; FOUNDER OF CLEAN SEAS

Afroz Shah, a young Indian lawyer from Mumbai, is synonymous with the world's largest beach clean-up project. So far, the volunteers have collected over 4,000 tons of trash from the 2.5-kilometre beach.

Every weekend since, Shah has inspired volunteers to join him—from slum-dwellers to Bollywood stars, from school children to politicians. They have been turning up at Versova for what Shah calls 'a date with the ocean', but what in reality means labouring shin-deep in rotting garbage under the scorching Indian sun.

He vows to continue his beach clean-up crusade until people and governments around the world change their approach to producing, using, and discarding plastic and other products that wash up onto beaches all over the world. Presently his mission is to clean the Mithi River, the main source of Mumbai's drinking water resources.

Looking at all these people, I wonder what prevents many more Indian-Muslims from becoming successful entrepreneurs. There are a multitude of small to fairly large businesses run by Indian-Muslims, but apart from a handful of successful Indian-Muslim businessmen none have reached the global stage yet.

> *'As the different streams having their sources in different places all mingle their water in the sea, so, O Lord, the different paths which people take through different tendencies, various though they appear, crooked or straight, all lead to Thee.'*
> *- Swami Vivekananda*

SECTION VI

A MINORITY'S MYSTIC MAJORITY

Muslims today represent a population of one hundred seventy-two million individuals, who profoundly contribute to the cultural vitality and demographic vibrancy of India on a daily basis. This number represents the second-largest critical mass of Muslims in any nation in the world. First and foremost, as Indian-Muslims, we should feel tremendous pride, a sense of empowerment and responsibility in this fact, because we serve as the trajectory to the compass of achievement for all Muslims in the world. The age-old saying of 'safety in numbers' is only partially true, there is also an 'inspiration in numbers'. This social responsibility should serve as the spark for the guiding light that is ingrained in the daily mentality of all Indian-Muslims.

Although one hundred seventy-two million is unquestionably a formidable number given India's vast population, this number 'only' represents 14.2% of the populace. The reason for these quotation marks has fundamentally to do with human nature's resigned acceptance of the definitions of the term's 'majority' and 'minority'. Generally, the first notion that enters an individual's mind when exposed to these terms is a purely quantitative phenomenon. Namely, we immediately define majority as greater than 50% of a whole, and similarly minority as less than 50% of a whole. However, narrowly viewing these concepts purely in the quantitative realm has profound consequences because it is fundamentally inaccurate.

Most importantly, we are making a deep assumption in defining these terms. We assume the 'whole' is a homogeneous society of individuals or elements, each with uniform access to the exact same resources. Thus, if all elements are identical, the number of elements is the sole determining factor in any decision. However, very few societies in the real world are strictly homogeneous, and thus it's invalid to use our preconceived quantitative notions. So, what do the majority and minority mean in the cases of a complex, delicate, and interrelated society of citizens? In any real-world heterogeneous society or organization, we tend to think of the majority as strong and the minority as weak. But at a more underlying level of consciousness, what we're really connoting is that the majority is understood as having power of influence and the minority as lacking in this power.

Let's look at a few examples of heterogeneous

organizations across sectors to inspect this more intimate understanding. In sports, the captain of a cricket team has a great deal of influence on the organization of players in the field, their positioning and batting order, and the overall strategy of how a cricket game is played and managed. A cricket team is made up of eleven players, and yet this one player is clearly stronger than all other ten combined. Thus, even though the rest of the team outnumbers a single player, the captain is the majority and the other ten players are minorities. In business, the CEO or MD of a company of several thousands of employees controls the company's long-term strategy, short-term operations, employee benefits, and the overall state of health. Here again, one individual controls the livelihood of thousands, and even though this one individual is outnumbered, he/she is the majority.

Finally, in socioeconomics, the wealthiest citizens of any country are a very small percentage of the population and yet have a significant power of influence. For example, in the United States as of 2018, 1% of the population controlled 47% of the wealth and 80% of the population controlled only 7% of the wealth. Given that only 1% of the population controlled almost half the nation's wealth, this 1% has a significant influence over meaningful policy such as taxation rates, political elections, job creation and health insurance. This 1% is clearly a majority.[30]

In all the cases above, we see that power of influence outweighs the deficiency in number. This power of influence is a by-product of talent, wealth, or positions of importance. Thus, as Indian-Muslims, we need to recognize that 172 million individuals can certainly serve as a majority if garnered with the appropriate power of influence.

Today, as we have already discussed earlier, Muslims in India identify being second-class citizens with very little influence, and view themselves as working, living, and raising families as minorities in a foreign land. So, the logical question becomes, how does this mentality change? More specifically, how are talent, wealth, or positions of importance achieved? In the spirit of the Harvard Business School model for justifying an answer, let's analyse a very notable case study. I can think of no case more wondrously successful of a small quantitative group ubiquitously classified as a majority, than the Jewish population in the United States.

Jewish Americans are widely regarded as a significant demographic power base responsible for steering and influencing socio-economic policy of the world's lone superpower. However, the Jewish American population is approximately 5.6 million or only 1.8% of the US population. Therefore, it's imperative that we delve into the pillars responsible for allowing Jewish America to acquire the requisite talent, wealth, and positions of importance necessary to exercise a substantial power of influence.

The first such pillar is unequivocally education. In general, the Jewish American population has not only made it an imperative priority, but a desperate necessity to acquire postgraduate education. For instance, while

27% of Americans have acquired postgraduate education, this number soars to 59% for Jewish Americans. Not coincidentally, there seems to be a direct correlation between education and income level. Most notably, 46% of Jewish Americans report family incomes of over USD 100,000 compared to 19% of all Americans. As we move to an ever more technologically dependent world, one that requires a very specific and detailed skill set, the only true world currency will continue to be education. This is a sentiment Jewish America has recognized now for several decades. By contrast, as we have previously dissected, regardless of age, gender, or subculture, Muslim India has abysmal graduation rates and the disheartening title of being the religious community with the lowest participation percentage of formal sector employment.

The second such pillar is a united revered and proactive network. According to the National Population Survey of 2001, 4.3 million Jewish Americans have either a strong religious or cultural connection to the Jewish community. Among these 4.3 million, 80% are described as 'strongly connected' to Judaism, indulging in active engagement with the religion. Furthermore, the 2008 American Religious Identification Survey found that approximately 3.4 million Jewish Americans consider themselves religious, out of a total Jewish American population of 5.4 million, amounting to 63%. But why are the aforementioned statistics a relevant component to acquiring talent, wealth, and positions of importance? In addition to Synagogues serving the purpose of worship, they are also mechanisms for professional networking and ascension. Since such concentrated amounts of Jewish Americans convene in the same place on a periodic basis, relationships are cultivated at a faster rate, with greater coverage and with higher intensity than otherwise. As we can all attest, religious ideology is a powerfully motivating mechanism in maintaining long-term meaningful connections as the common denominator of relatable beliefs leads to trust in the form of business alliances and assistance.

The final pillar is an unwavering commitment to enhancing the infrastructure of this network through dedicated contributions of money, time, and ideas, ensuring a legacy of continuous excellence. Jewish America heavily prioritizes reinvestment in the educational and cultural fostering of the next generation in the form of foundations, scholarships, endowments, and non-profit programs. In 2007, *Forbes* magazine specifically featured 12 Jewish foundations within its list of the Top 200 charities in the United States. The average net assets of these foundations were almost USD 372 million. Furthermore, the average charitable commitment, a measure determining the percentage amount of a foundation's budget that goes directly to charitable services and not to other expenses such as operating costs and staff salaries, of these 12 foundations was 86%.

These above pillars are an illustration of the cataclysmic juxtaposition between today's Jewish America and Muslim India from the standpoint of meticulous execution of objectives, infiltration of corruption, and scale of impact.

Glaringly apparent to me is the necessity of having an apex independent body such as the IMSET. This organization appears to be the antidote for Muslim India's tearful yearning and can play a momentous role in creating progressive alignments for India's future.

I have excited confidence that one day Muslim India will even surpass the imprint of today's Jewish American empire. My profound admiration for this empire comes from its lateral expansion from scratch. The Jewish example is a beacon of hope; a compellingly inspirational tale of rising from the ashes like a phoenix regardless of the most gruesome racial, political, and territorial upheaval. We often forget that the extreme ethnic cleansing and genocide of millions of Jews that defines the Holocaust during World War II led to the widespread Jewish emigration into the United States in the late 1940s. Thus, the dominance of today's Jewish America has arisen at an alarmingly rapid rate in an incredibly short amount of time. Furthermore, these Jewish refugees came to America with no prior history of interaction with the nation, and in all but fifty years purely personified the moniker of the United States, namely, 'the land of opportunity'.

These are staggering statistics speaking to the enormity of contribution as well as the seamless operation of this contribution in reaching its intended purpose. By contrast, the share of Muslims as beneficiaries in Indian government programs ranges between 3-14%, which is much lower than their due share according to their population. The Integrated Child Development Services (ICDS) programs have not made any major headway and the coverage of Muslims under the scheme has been less than 8% when compared with the OBCs (13%) and SCs and STs (10%).

To meet the cost of several initiatives like the ICDS centres, JNNRUM, Sarva Shiksha Abhiyan, and Public Health Programs, a supplemental effort by way of human resource and material contribution has to come from beneficiaries through community participation. Increased allocation in the institutions of higher learning and provision of land for schools, playgrounds, and health institutions can be linked to the usufruct flowing from the Wakf properties inherited or set apart in perpetuity as an act of piety. Generous Muslims adhering to the principles of endowment bequeath valuable properties dedicated to meet the cost of maintenance of the poor or any charitable institution or even the bequeathed property itself. The total area under these Wakf properties is reported to be 600,000 acres, with an estimated market value worth 1.20 lakh crore, as of now, the revenue from rented properties is negligible at INR 8,000 crore, which is not even 1% of the actual rent value these properties can give. If these properties are leased out at market prices and developed with private partners, the rental income alone will be not less than INR 90,000 crore to INR 1 lakh crore per annum, though considerable portion of this endowment is under encroachment and illegal occupation, even those of the government departments.[31]

The above-mentioned Wakf board problems have been languishing in the hands of successive central governments for decades. The apathy and disregard for a large Muslim community shown by the past governments is really shameful and unforgivable. Though a central Wakf council under the Ministry of Social Justice and a Joint Parliamentary Committee on Wakfs does monitor the working of the State Wakf Boards, the performance of these boards has not yielded good results. Many valuable endowments have withered away and there is an urgent need for affirmative and prompt action.

Therefore, the recent announcement by the Modi government on finding a solution to this chronic problem, which was depriving a large Muslim population of their inherited rights, is a huge relief. Prime Minister Narendra Modi has rolled up his sleeves to tackle this matter with his characteristic determination, as evident in his words: 'Unfortunately, minorities of this country have been kept in fear, used in elections. We have to end this cycle. We have worked for 'Sabka Saath, Sabka Vikas', now we have to strive for 'Sabka Vishwas'. The ones who vote for us, are a part of us. The ones who don't, are also a part of us.[32]

As mentioned in the earlier chapter, I have confidence in the Prime Minister's vision and commitments, specially the digitalization of the age-old lingering problem of irregularities of the Wakf board's old records within a time period of hundred days. The government also has decided to develop these Wakf properties into skill development hubs called as 'Hunarmund'. While I welcome this, it is my personal view that the funds from these trusts should be also spent into IT technology institutes and medical centres for health care. This move will save the government a huge amount of money being spent from the consolidated fund of India.

Going by all this, of course, Muslim India has a tremendous advantage over today's Jewish America in that it has already experienced a library of accomplishment, a series of enduring trials and tribulations, and an intimately grandiose history with the country that it's attempting to resurrect a powerful presence. This familiarity will be the driving force of a time to come where we reflect on the obstacles of Muslim life's odyssey within the Indian soil, and recognize that it paved the way for halcyon days of peace and prosperity.

SECTION VII

THE GAME CHANGER

As we have emphatically witnessed, Muslims are an integral part of the country and our history is meticulously interwoven with the Indian heritage, which belongs to Muslims as much as it belongs to all socio-religious communities. Any sense of deprivation or perceived notion of deliberate discrimination needs to be meticulously addressed and for this the IMSET mechanism will go a long way in alleviating apprehensions with a view to remedy Indian-Muslim ailment. It's now time to lift this veil of conceptuality and extract the explicit vision for the IMSET.

The beauty of the Indian-Muslim Socio-Economic Trust will be in its seeming duality. It will be one hundred per cent in line with the Indian Constitution and simultaneously will not be affiliated with any political party or government or religious allegiance of any kind. This apolitical autonomy will be essential in maintaining the purity of excellence in education, medical, science, technology, banking, and legal services, and socio-economic guidance will be provided.

The IMSET will be a non-profit organization functioned via technology in the form of a digital application. A trained team of youngsters with complete knowledge and functioning of the digital app will guide it. This team will be monitored by an expert eminent committee for the community who will offer their services. It will engage pre-eminently successful Muslims in today's India from each state, which will include captains of industry and tycoons in their respective fields of expertise.

The IMSET app will be defined by a collaborative spirit and genuine empathy, as all the members will be invited to serve based on their seminal achievements and genetic inclination for volunteerism and social responsibility via video webinar, online meetings, trainings, and support. These positions will be highly prestigious, not due to the traditional business perks of compensation, rather due to the proximity of substantially impactful work. They will leave their indelible imprints on the sands of time and their heroic deeds will inspire generations to come.

The organization's operating budget will be based entirely on philanthropy and contributions and crowdfunding from the community. At its essence, the IMSET will be a symbol for creating a repetitive circle of contributing efforts. Board members, service recipients, and organizational stakeholders should feel compelled to maintain the thriving effectiveness of the IMSET via participation as a result of their positive experiences related to the organization. The benefits, guidance, and resources these individuals earn in order to thrive and prosper should compel them to in turn give back so the next generation's benefit can be as impactful from the recycling of these services. It is extremely important to note that there is no intention of the Trust to promote the Islamic religion; this body shall not be a religious organization, rather a charitable one, with the intention to support the underprivileged Muslims for their economic, social, and educational well-being. From the standpoint of educational services, we need to reshape the conversation to one of competitiveness, so Muslim students are on an equal footing with everyone else.

The Trust will create intensive coaching programs, preparing and motivating students for competitive examinations, especially for those veering towards the Civil Services with the help of video webinars and the experts committed in the specific locality. These programs will hire established faculty, via the IMSET's operating budget, and maintain a low student-to-faculty ratio in order to ensure students are getting the dedicated and personalized attention they need.

These programs will be absolutely free for the students they serve. Furthermore, the Trust will provide a plethora of scholarship opportunities for such under-represented, low-income, first-generation college-bound Muslim students, both men and women, to fund their education, specifically their tuition, books, and supplies. Muslim women should be encouraged to engage themselves shoulder to shoulder with men to keep their equality and share of education and positions. Muslim women should aspire to help each other to carve out their rightful place in society on an equal footing with the men including taking a leadership role in all fields. However, it's not enough to simply have students pass entrance examinations and have the resources to begin their educational careers. Educational access is only the first half of our goal; the other half will be what becomes part of his being.

Once students have reached the colleges of their choice and have the financial means to complete their degrees, they must have the toolkit to specifically do so. Thus, the IMSET will conduct seminars on career guidance, counselling, and mentorship for its students online via high-end video streaming. These opportunities will range from how to construct effective resumes for prospective employers, how to prepare for professional interviews, and dedicated tutoring in courses of difficulty. Furthermore, a significant aspect of the IMSET's educational initiative will be one of mentorship. Matching rising students with established professionals will be a vital aspect for the IMSET's students to understand the practical real-world challenges and responsibilities associated with success. The students will have the opportunity, with the help of video webinar real-life conversations with their respective mentors, to ask questions related to career paths, directions of opportunities, and cultures of companies. This would give them the type of implicit education one cannot receive strictly in the classroom.

It is envisaged that once the IMSET gets established and settled we propose to take the following plan to the next level.

In the area of banking, the IMSET will aim to set up a bank with the objective of cultivating growth in entrepreneurial ventures and small businesses. The funds for setting up the bank will be initially contributed by the community in small donations till such time the bank stabilizes its operations. The IMSET banking will benefit the small Muslim entrepreneurs. The IMSET bank will provide interest-free loans for aspiring Muslims to start businesses, contingent upon meeting explicit IMSET criteria. Namely, these businesses must pass a review determining profitability.

We will reason with companies in India to not reject job applications to deserving Muslim candidates who possess explicit educational qualifications for the requisite job and not to deprecate them for being a member of their community. Employment will provide an overall benefit to the nation's economy.

Furthermore, students who may not qualify for IMSET scholarships will have the opportunity to apply for an interest-free loan to complete their education. The IMSET will endeavour in an incentivized model similar to the United States—students that are able to secure certain prestigious employments within the public sector will have the opportunity to have the outstanding loan amount pardoned. The vision being that students and professionals who receive the generosity of such services will undoubtedly reciprocate to the IMSET's financial viability.

From a legal perspective, the IMSET will provide pro-bono representation for any of its members to ensure fair practices and operations in all academic and professional sectors. This is a necessary component to ensure events such as the devaluing and mismanagement of the Wakf properties discussed earlier are avoided in the name of protecting the weak. Additionally, the IMSET's intrinsic approach to legally questionable and 'grey area' circumstances will be purely Gandhian.

The final component of the IMSET's core agenda will be that of offering high-quality medical services to all Muslims, free of charge. The IMSET will execute large-scale fundraising campaigns to generate the capital investment required to build hospitals and health care centres. These facilities will have the most cutting-edge technology ensuring the most superior healthcare for all disadvantaged Muslims. This Socialist approach to healthcare is rooted in the fundamentally humane notion that all individuals, regardless of social, economic or material status, have the right to be equal in the dignity of their vitality. This is a dignity impossible to exercise without the presence of good health. Furthermore, treatment cannot be the only emphasis to truly thriving healthcare; the idea of prevention must be embedded in its rudiments. In that vein, the Trust will create a customized curriculum of health and hygiene awareness seminars that will be deployed all throughout the nation, so there is a greater understanding for all Muslims to eliminate the behavioural causes of poor health. This will give a great push in helping to resolve the exponential rise in deteriorating health care conditions in the country. This contribution will strengthen the hand of the government.

From a day-to-day operational standpoint, the IMSET will conduct social awareness studies on current real issues confronting certain segments of the Muslim population in order to understand how the organization can better serve its constituents. These studies will involve collecting, compiling, and analysing data, packaging the results in a comprehensible manner for the IMSET's board to provide strategic action. These issues can have an infinite range; yet will be harnessed by the quality of life for Indian-Muslims.

It is my fervent hope that the Muslim youth, in particular, take full advantage of the IMSET by stepping out to the frontline and immersing themselves in academic, social, and extracurricular activities in order to have a multipronged perspective essential to claiming a rightful place as a leader of tomorrow. I want our Indian-Muslim youth to also be aware of the evil forces around them, namely, taking friendship in the name of brotherhood and then being misguided off the path of success. They must prepare themselves for any challenges and wholeheartedly participate with our Hindu brothers and sisters, as well as from other religions, in a spirit of cooperation and Indianness. After all, we share the same country and it is our moral duty to protect not only our social order and economy but also to protect our motherland from any enemy within or out.

The IMSET is entrusted to provide our Muslim youth with the necessary road signs to stay on the right path. But the IMSET is dedicated to the prosperity of Muslims of all ages, regions, and genders. I no longer want to endure the overwhelming pain of seeing a Muslim beggar, a human so desperate in an entrapped plight that the regard for self-humiliation is voluntarily ignored.

The IMSET is about regaining pride and dignity in a people presently hollow of it. The Trust is not about religion, it's about purity; it's not about Hindus and Muslims, it's about humanity. As Maulana Abul Kalam Azad dictated in his illuminating treatise, *Ghubar-e-Khatir*, 'the pluralistic feature of Indian cultural heritage to which Muslims have contributed substantially, proves that no part of India could be described as holy or unholy'. As Mahatma Gandhi, in his prayer meeting at Rajghat on March 24th, 1947, pointedly referenced Sir Syed Ahmad Khan's famous averment, 'Hindus and Muslims are the two eyes of a bride and the trouble in one eye will hurt the other also'. He made it abundantly clear that though the Muslims came to India from distant lands, they adopted this land as their own, grew up for centuries with others with a sense of unity, shared their joys and sorrows, and produced a happy synthesis that no diabolic designs can ever break. History has proved right from the dawn of time that the oppressors have always lost in the end. My personal view is that to move this country to its glorious heights we need the unity, strength, and dedication of all of its people.

I know it won't be easy, but I am inherently committed to dedicating the rest of my life initiating the IMSET from concept to completion. At this point, I can't help but revert back to Tipu Sultan, as much of my professional life has been indelibly intertwined with his persona. Tipu Sultan was a great secular Indian, a man who never surrendered his principles in the defence of his motherland.

The entire Muslim community should seriously introspect their position. The prevailing conditions of today's Muslims are fast deteriorating into an abyss of darkness. We are living under false bravado and self-deception that all is well. If only you look at the status of education, employment, business, and facilities available to Indian-Muslims, you will realize the plight and the false emptiness we are living in. It is my firm belief that once the IMSET is established with a strong structural organization then it will become the bedrock of inspiration, guidance, and leadership. It is left up to us fortunate Muslims to lead by example and philanthropy and uplift our brethren to help them achieve a desired socio-economic status and their rightful place in society.

An educated community is an enlightened one. The insight I have given you into the Jewish community's extraordinary efforts to come together, help each other, and consolidate their position has propelled them to one of the successful communities in the world, both socially and economically. Thus I ask the more fortunate amongst my community whom Allah has blessed with power and wealth to come forward magnanimously in making and sustaining the Trust.

My message to the government of India is simple: it's high time to end the empty philosophical rhetoric and act. In no way am I resigning myself to simply preaching these bold statements, rather I am glueing these ideological mantras to the systematic and strategic creation of the Trust. A digital application, I believe that will address the causality of these ubiquitous yet ruinous issues, will create a solution through a sustainable legacy of prosperity and inspire the government to assist in formulating subsequent services for its continuous benefit.

However, from the Muslim perspective, we need to purge the notion that India is a country that we are simply living in, working in, and trying to survive in.

So aptly conveyed by Sukh Deo Muni in *Quartz* India: 'Those on the quest for narrow political gains overlook the fact that India assimilated Islam and made it more positive compared to its Wahabi aspect. India's Barelvi and Deobandi theological schools and the Sufi variant of Islam's teachings gave it a new and broader interpretation. India also played a key role in taking Islam to Southeast Asia where it stands as a moderate faith compared to its radicalised version wreaking havoc in Pakistan and West Asia.'[33]

India can take a lead in owning Islam and projecting its softer Sufi version in countering the radical Jihadi thrust that fuels terrorism ideologically. There is considerable potential for India to develop the Islamic tourism sector as well.

Through a detailed breakdown of the mission, structure, and operation of this Trust, I passionately and pragmatically intend to convince and inspire our Indian-Muslims to attain the pinnacles of education to elevate themselves to a position of respect, in the process joining mainstream India and becoming contributing citizens to the exchequer.

This should provide a very tangible, explicit, and logical solution for Muslims in India to once again reach the zenith of the contribution of impact left by them over the centuries. This is the impact that Muslims in India have repeatedly accomplished in the past while forming the rich history of this amazingly unique country. As we have already explored, Muslims have selflessly contributed an immense amount to India, from the standpoint of art, architecture, science, technology, and governance, making India the richest country in the world. These timeless, priceless, and permanent contributions make India just as much *ours* as anyone else's. We are not immigrants of this country; we are the sons and daughters of the soil. It's time my fellow brothers and sisters reclaim that spirit of the soil.

BIBLIOGRAPHY

1. NL Team. 2019. "India will have largest Muslim population in the world in 2060, but Muslims will remain religious minority: Pew Research." newslaundry.com. April 5. https://www.newslaundry.com/shorts/india-will-have-largest-muslim-population-in-the-world-in-2060-but-muslims-will-remain-religious-minority-pew-research
2. Sen Nag, Oishimaya. 2019. "Muslim Population By Country." WorldAtlas. March 8. https://www.worldatlas.com/articles/countries-with-the-largest-muslim-populations.html
3. Wolfe, Daniel, Dan Kopf, and Aria Thaker. 2019. "Why is Muslim political representation declining in India?" qz.com. May 22. https://qz.com/india/1617067/indian-election-2019-why-few-muslims-make-it-to-the-lok-sabha/

Bibliography

4. Khan, Sanjay. 2018. *The Best Mistakes of My Life: Autobiography of Sanjay Khan.* India: Penguin India.
5. Safvi, Rana. 2018. "If Mughals did not loot India, what exactly was their contributions?" Daily O. January 26. https://www.dailyo.in/variety/rajputs-mughal-empire-india-economy-medieval-india-british-raj-1857-revolt/story/1/21997.html
6. Maddison, Angus. 2007. *Contours of the World Economy, 1–2030 AD: Essays in Macro-economic History.* New Delhi: Oxford University Press.
7. Maddison, Angus. 2001. *The World Economy: A Millennial Perspective.* Development Centre Studies. Paris: OECD Publishing. https://doi.org/10.1787/9789264189980-en.
8. Safvi, Rana. 2017. "No, Mughals didn't loot India. They made us rich." Daily O. September 16. https://www.dailyo.in/politics/mughals-contribution-indian-economy-rich-culture-tourism-british/story/1/19549.html
9. Habib, Irfan, ed. 2002. *Confronting Colonialism Resistance and Modernization under Haidar Ali and Tipu Sultan.* India: Anthem Press.
10. Das, Subhamoy. 2018. "30 Quotes In Praise of India." Learn Religions. September 2. https://www.learnreligions.com/quotes-in-praise-of-india-1770404
11. Violatti, Cristian. 2013. "Chanakya." Ancient History Encyclopedia. November 3. https://www.ancient.eu/Kautilya/

12. Bhattacharya, Sukumar. "THE MEN WHO RULED INDIA, 1899—1901 (A Sketch by Lord Curzon)." *Proceedings of the Indian History Congress* 18 (1955): 209-16. http://www.jstor.org/stable/44137388.
13. Bhattacharya, Sukumar. "THE MEN WHO RULED INDIA, 1899—1901 (A Sketch by Lord Curzon)." *Proceedings of the Indian History Congress* 18 (1955): 209-16. http://www.jstor.org/stable/44137388.
14. Cabinet Secretariat, Government of India. 2006. "Social, Economic and Educational Status of the Muslim Community of India – Report." November. https://mhrd.gov.in/sites/upload_files/mhrd/files/sachar_comm.pdf
15. Special Correspondent. 2018. "Govt reports 27% rise in communal clashes." The Telegraph – Online Edition. July 27. https://www.telegraphindia.com/india/govt-reports-27-rise-in-communal-clashes/cid/1352345
16. Parker, Priya. 2006. "Summary of Sachar committee Report." https://www.prsindia.org/administrator/uploads/general/1242304423~~Summary%20of%20Sachar%20Committee%20Report.pdf
17. Khan, Intakhab. 2016. "Muslim Education in Post-Independence – Issues, Factors, and Prospects." ResearchGate. January. https://www.researchgate.net/publication/299388863_Muslim_Education_in_Post-Independent_India_-Issues_Factors_and_Prospects
18. D. Bengalee, Dr. Mehroo. 2007. Research Project

Report on All India Birth Rate of Parsi – Zoroastrians from 2001 till 15th August, 2007. National Commission For Minorities, Government Of India. http://ncm.nic.in/pdf/Parsi%20%20Report.pdf

19. 2017. "With 27% of world GDP, India was the richest country under Muslim Rule: Shashi Tharoor." ummid.com News Network. October 20. https://www.ummid.com/news/2017/October/20.10.2017/shashi-tharoor-on-indias-gdp-under-muslim-rule.html

20. Narula, Manju. 2014. "Educational Development of Muslim Minority: With Special Reference to Muslim Concentrated States of India." *Journal of Education and Research* 4(1): 93-108. doi:10.3126/jer.v4i1.10729

21. Sikand, Yogendra. 2005. "Reforming the Indian Madrassas: Contemporary Muslim Voices." *Bastions of the Believers. Madrasas and Islamic Education in India.* New Delhi: Penguin India.

22. Reddy, Vinodh. 2017. Fundamental Rights (Articles 14-18, 19-22, 23-24, 25-28, 29-30, 32). Edu General. https://edugeneral.org/blog/polity/fundamental-rights-articles-14-18-19-22-23-24-25-28-29-30-32/

23. IANS. 2019. "Govt to roll out steps to modernise 'madrassa' education next month." The Economic Times. June 11. https://economictimes.indiatimes.com/news/politics-and-nation/govt-to-roll-out-steps-to-modernise-madrassa-education-next-month/articleshow/69744355.cms?from=mdr

24. Hasan, Zoya, and Ritu Menon. 2005. *Educating Muslim Girls: A Comparison of Five Indian Cities.* New Delhi: Women Unlimited.
25. Kazi, Seema. 1999. "Muslim Women in India." Minority Rights Group. February. https://cdn.atria.nl/epublications/1999/MuslimwomenIndia.pdf
26. Shakdher, *Education Commissions and Committees in Restrospect, Opcit., p.25. Ibid.*, p.28. G.O.Ms.No.451, Education, 01.04.1964. Saraswathi *op.cit.*, p. 308. *Ibid.*, p.310., DEVELOPMENT OF MUSLIM EDUCATION Mohamed Shafique Zaman, Problems of Minorities' Education, Book links Corporation, Hyderabad, 2001, p. 16.
27. Dimitripoulou, Alexandra. 2019. "Countries With The Most Women Business Owners As A Percentage Of Total Business Owners, 2018." CEOworld Magazine. January 21. https://ceoworld.biz/2019/01/21/countries-with-the-most-women-business-owners-as-a-percentage-of-total-business-owners-2018/
28. Khan, Intakhab. 2016. "Muslim education in Post-Independence India — Issues, Factors and Prospects." ResearchGate. January. https://www.researchgate.net/publication/299388863_Muslim_Education_in_Post-Independent_India_-Issues_Factors_and_Prospects
29. 2002. "Muslim Women's Survey." infochange.com. December. http://infochangeindia.org/women/189-women/books-a-reports/5891-muslim-womens-survey

30. Treanor, Jill. 2015. "Half of world's wealth now in hands of 1% of population – report." theguardian.com. October 13. https://www.theguardian.com/money/2015/oct/13/half-world-wealth-in-hands-population-inequality-report
31. Pandey, Maneesh. 2013. "Value of Wakf properties in six major metros pegged at Rs 1.5 lakh crore." India Today. August 23. https://www.indiatoday.in/india/north/story/value-of-wakf-properties-in-six-major-metros-minority-affairs-ministry-k-rehman-kha-174670-2013-08-23
32. Kidwai, Rasheed. 2019. "Muslim community leaders reaching for engagement with Modi 2.0 government." Observer research foundation. May 28. https://www.orfonline.org/expert-speak/muslim-community-leaders-reaching-engagement-modi-2-0-government-51395/
33. Deo Muni, Sukh. 2018. "Why Islam must be made part of India's foreign policy." Quartz India. June 29. https://qz.com/india/1317840/modi-must-make-islam-a-part-of-indias-foreign-policy/

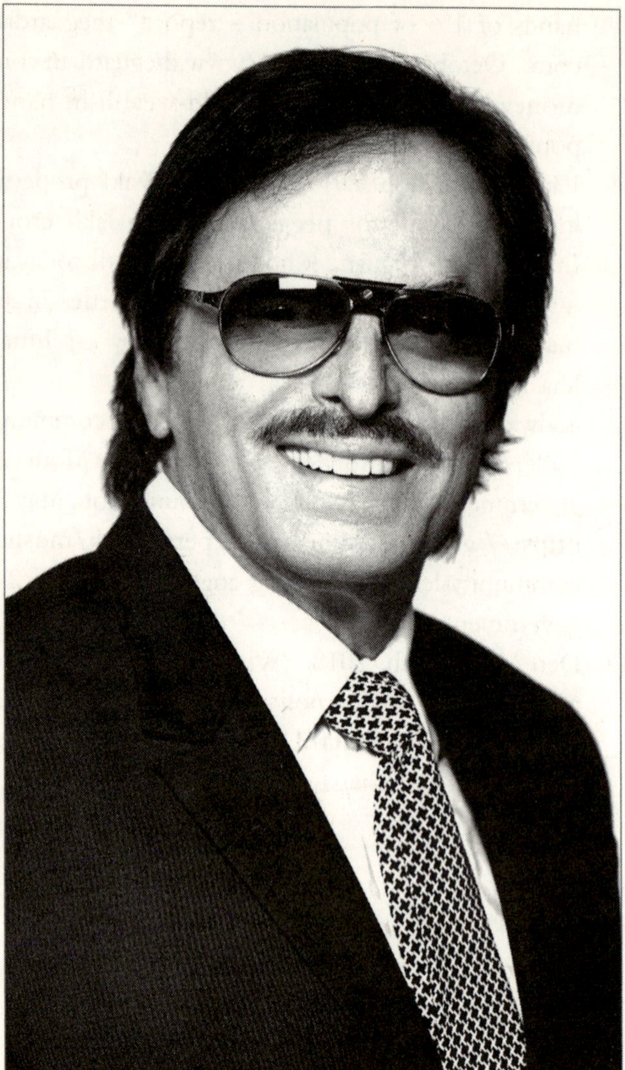

Sanjay Khan is a renowned actor, director, producer, respected and much-loved for his work done in the space of Hindi cinema and the Indian television industry. He has directed and acted in movies like like *Dosti*, *Dus Lakh*, *Ek Phool Do Mali*, *Intaqam*, *Dhund*, *Mela* and directed mega-serials like *The Sword of Tipu Sultan*, *the Great Maratha*, and *Jai Hanuman*.

Mr Khan has been awarded and felicitated numerously throughout his career. Some of his recognitions include, Uttar Pradesh Film Journalists Association Award (1981), Andhra Pradesh Journalist Award (1986), The Gem of India Award for Excellence (1993), The Rajiv Gandhi Excellence Award (1993), The Udyog Ratna Gold Medal Award (1994), The Aashirwad Award (1994), The Arch of Excellence Award (1994), National Citizen's Award (1994), The Glory of India Award (1995), The Super Achiever of India Award (1995), Hind Gaurav Award (1997), Kashi Pandit Sansad Award, Business Initiation Development Award (1997), Honour of Lifetime Achiever Award (1996), Achiever of Millennium Award (1999), The Millennium Achievers (2000), American Federation of Muslims of Indian Origin (2006), and the Lifetime Achievement Award by Screen Star (2009).

He is also the author of *The Best Mistakes of my Life* (Penguin Random House, 2018). *Assalamualaikum Watan* is his second book.

To know more about him, visit www.sanjaykhanofficial.com.